FATHERS AND SONS

Russia at the Cross-roads

Edward Wasiolek

TWAYNE PUBLISHERS • NEW YORK
Maxwell Macmillan Canada • *Toronto*
Maxwell Macmillan International • *New York Oxford Singapore Sydney*

Twayne's Masterwork Studies No. 101

Copyright 1993 by Twayne Publishers
All rights reserved. No part of this book may be reproduced or transmitted in any form
or by any means, electronic or mechanical, including photocopying, recording, or by
any information storage and retrieval system, without permission in writing from the
Publisher.

Twayne Publishers	Maxwell Macmillan Canada, Inc.
Macmillan Publishing Company	1200 Eglinton Avenue East
866 Third Avenue	Suite 200
New York, New York 10022	Don Mills, Ontario M3C 3N1

Macmillan Publishing Company is a part of the Maxwell Communication Group of
Companies.

Library of Congress Cataloging-in-Publication Data
Wasiolek, Edward.
  Fathers and Sons : Russia at the cross-roads / Edward Wasiolek.
      p.   cm.—(Twayne's masterwork studies ; 101)
  Includes bibliographical references and index.
  ISBN 0-8057-9445-X—ISBN 0-8057-8598-1 (pbk.)
    1. Turgenev, Ivan Sergeevich, 1818–1883. Ottsy i deti. I. Title. II. Series.
PG4320.083W37   1993
891.73'3—dc20   93-15743
                                                                          CIP

The paper used in this publication meets the minimum requirements of American
National Standard for Information Sciences—Permanence of Paper for Printed Library
Materials, ANSI Z39.48-1984.∞™

10 9 8 7 6 5 4 3 2 1 (alk. paper)
10 9 8 7 6 5 4 3 2 1 (pbk.: alk. paper)

Printed in the United States of America.

Contents

Note on the References

Quotations from *Fathers and Sons* are from Bernard Guilbert Guerney's translation of Turgenev's novel (New York: The Modern Library, 1961). Guerney's translation is by far the best English translation; he is faithful to the original, and his English is contemporary, idiomatic, and stylistically impeccable. Guerney has rendered this Russian into comparable English: Turgenev's Russian is clear, simple, and effortless to read.

Ivan Turgenev.

Chronology: Ivan Turgenev's Life and Works

1818   Ivan Turgenev born in Orel, 300 miles southwest of Moscow and halfway to Kiev, to a family of great wealth. The family estate, Spasskoe, is a self-sufficient kingdom, with 5,000 serfs, 30 villages, 30 acres of gardens and parks, and its own tannery and wallpaper-making shop. The family has its own doctor, orchestra, singers, actors, tutors, governesses.

1833   Enters the University of Moscow. Among his contemporaries are V. G. Belinsky and Alexander Gertsen.

1834   Enters the University of St. Petersburg.

1838–1841   Studies philosophy at the University of Berlin.

1843   Publishes *Parasha* at his own expense. Meets Pauline García Viardot, who is destined to be the love of his life. Spanish by origin and French by domicile, Viardot is a famous opera singer.

1847–1852   Begins publishing a series of short sketches of Russian village life that are collected under the title *Notes of a Hunter* (sometimes translated as *A Sportsman's Sketches*) in 1852.

1850   Mother, Barbara Petrovna, dies. "Diary of a Superfluous Man" published. Finishes *A Month in the Country*.

1852–1853   Gets in trouble with the authorities by making some indiscreet comments in an obituary on Gogol; is exiled to his estate for a couple of years.

1855   *Rudin* and *Faust*.

1856   Leaves Russia to live in Europe, where he stays for the rest of his life, except for intermittent returns to Russia.

1857   Publishes "Asya," which is sharply criticized by N. K. Chernyshevsky in "The Russian Man at a Romantic Tryst."

Chronology

LITERARY AND HISTORICAL CONTEXT

1

Historical Background

Fathers and Sons (1862) was written in 1860–61, an important and tumultuous period in Russian history. After the death of Czar Nicholas I in 1856 and the ascension of Alexander II, the most important social question in Russia was the liberation of the serfs. All progressive opinion was united on this issue, and it was determined that the serfs be liberated. This was accomplished by the emperor's decree in 1861. *Fathers and Sons* was not only written in the very crucible of this debate, but it also summarizes in fictive form much of the debate about Russia's future that had gone on in the 1850s.

Russian national consciousness was slow in maturing in the early decades of the nineteenth century. After the war with Napoleon in 1812, Russia was invaded by Western ideas that had been brought back by the troops occupying France. During the 1820s and 1830s Russian thought was influenced powerfully by several waves of German Romantic idealism and then the philosophy of Hegel, both of which raised to Russian consciousness the concept of distinct national identity and of "inevitable" historical progress.

After the Napoleonic war a palace revolution took place in December 1925 by the so-called Decembrists, a group of army officers and distinguished nobles that agitated for some limitation of Russia's absolute monarchy. The revolution was a failure, and the participants were exiled to Siberia. A period of repression ensued until the mid-1850s, when, in the aftermath of the lost Crimean War (1854–56) and the advent of Alexander II, important reforms, such as the emancipation of the serfs, were instituted.

Much of this demand for social change came from a new class of obstreperous social activists known as the generation of the 1850s and 1860s because they are usually set against the generation of the 1830s and 1840s. The latter generation (the fathers) was for the most part liberal aristocrats (Turgenev was one of them) who, under the influence of German idealistic thought, did a great deal of talking and theorizing about social change without going from thought and talk to action. These "liberals"—among them V. G. Belinsky, Alexander Herzen, T. N. Granovsky, and Turgenev himself—wanted the abolition of serfdom, some limitation on the power of the autocracy, and some constitutional change.[1] They wanted the changes to take place gradually, within the framework of the monarchy and probably with some preservation of their aristocratic privileges. A good characterization of this generation can be found in Herzen's *My Past and Times* (1852–55), and they are satirized in Dostoyevski's portrait of Stepan Trofimovich in *The Possessed* (1869).

The ideological sons of these liberal fathers—the generation of the 1850s and 1860s—were different in class origin, in manners, and in demands. They were for the most part not aristocrats but university-educated people, whose fathers were priests, bureaucrats, and liberated peasants. Called *raznochintsy* (of varied class), they were tired of talk; they wanted radical reform and were committed to violence, if necessary, to achieve these reforms. They attacked not only the political and economic conditions but also art and the relations between men and women—indeed, the whole structure of man's psychological and spiritual being. They were brash, coarse, arrogant, uncompromising, and extremely talented. They were very young, all in their twenties, and they had nothing but contempt for their liberal predecessor fathers. The most talented of the group was the intellectual and critic N. K. Chernyshevsky, who today is one of the saints in the Russian gallery of great men.[2] His two most brilliant disciples, Nikolay Dobrolyubov and Dmitri Pisarev, took his thinking to extremes. The words and ideas of these three are the sources for much of Bazarov's thoughts and actions.

Such distinguished writers as Dostoyevski and Tolstoy were writing during these years. A committed enemy of all liberalism and radicalism, Dostoyevski had little good to say about the "fathers" or the "sons." Tolstoy had an Olympian indifference to the political currents of the time. Both men had, in their early years, flirted with liberalism and radicalism. Tolstoy had considerable interaction with some of the liberal groups in the 1850s, and Dostoyevski was arrested for conspiratorial activities in 1849 and imprisoned and exiled for 10 years. Both men were "conservatives" and, with such people as N. N. Strakhov, Afanasi Fet, Apollon Grigor'ev, and Mikhail Katkov, formed a third ideological grouping.

Pavel Kirsanov is a representative of the liberals of the 1830s and 1840s, and Bazarov is a representative of the radicals of the 1850s and 1860s. The debate is between those who believe in tradition, gradual change, and unconscious forces as the most effective development of Russia's history and those who believe in reason, science, and conscious and willed direction and manipulation of development. *Fathers and Sons* embodies in very powerful form a dialogue that had been going on since the beginning of Russia's national consciousness. It is a debate that implies two distinct views of life: one that sees man commanded by forces he can discern but cannot control, and another that sees man as the architect of his own history and destiny.

One form of the debate has to do with how Russia was to pursue its national development—by relying on its own spiritual forces or by taking over the ideas and social schemes of the West—a debate traditionally characterized as the argument between the Westerners and the Slavophiles, between those who favor following the path of European rationalism and technological development and those who believe that Russia has a unique path of fidelity to forces greater than reason and technology. The argument goes back at least to the eighteenth century and Peter the Great's decision to open Russia to the West. He forbade some of the ancient customs, encouraged knowledge and learning about the West, and symbolically moved the capital from the interior of Russia (Moscow) to the margins of Europe in St. Petersburg.

In Tolstoy's *War and Peace* (1866–69) it is Moscow and the traditional resources of the Russian people that defeat Napoleon, whereas St. Petersburg, the foreign Western city, is a hotbed of intrigue favoring peace with Napoleon. At the beginning of the twentieth century the battle between Westernism and Slavophilism took the form of a struggle between Tolstoyanism, which represented a wholesale rejection of technology and Western rationalism, and Marxism, an ideology that championed a rational and technological development. Significantly, Marxism is a Western import to Russia. The ideological collisions in *Fathers and Sons* reach deep into the history of Russian thought and the Russian psyche.

2

The Importance of *Fathers and Sons*

Fathers and Sons is Turgenev's best work and one of Russia's classics. No selection of great Russian fiction would be complete without it. Its title and its main character have become archetypal for Russian literature. The theme of generational conflict is obsessive in Russian literature. *Fathers and Sons* is deeply embedded in the Russian imagination, in the way that Huckleberry Finn is embedded in America's. Huck pushing off from the shore, away from the constraints of family, school, church, and civil institutions onto the free and unpredictable currents of the Mississippi reenacts the American fascination with the frontier and the freedom and individualism demanded by frontier conditions. *Fathers and Sons* deals with the conflict of generations, which in turn raises the issue of where Russia is going and where it should go. No nation's literature is more obsessed with the issue of national identity and national destiny. Bazarov and the image he raises of a new society and a new man represent a powerful act of imagining what Russia and human society can be.

Both Mark Twain's novel and *Fathers and Sons* are also powerful as works of art. There is hardly a character in Russian literature that has so powerfully impressed itself on the reader's imagination as has Bazarov. The other characters too—Odintsova and the Kirsanovs—are also powerfully drawn. The language is pure, simple, and clear, reminding one of the style of Russia's national poet, Aleksandr Pushkin. Turgenev has an uncanny ability to raise profound and complex issues with a light and transparent touch. Both Henry James and Ernest Hemingway looked to him as a master craftsman, the former, a demanding critic, calling him "the novelist's novelist" in his essay "Turgenev and Tolstoy."

Fathers and Sons appeared at an extraordinary moment in Russian letters. Indeed, no decade has been as literarily rich as was the decade of the 1860s in Russia. Dostoyevski published *Notes from the Underground* in 1864, *Crime and Punishment* in 1866, *The Idiot* in 1868, and *The Possessed* in 1869; Leo Tolstoy was to publish *War and Peace* between 1866 and 1869. In addition to *Fathers and Sons* (1862), Turgenev had published three important novels in the second half of the 1850s.

Turgenev was able to respond to the period's social change, civic turmoil, and intense ideological struggle by giving us a condensed image of that historical moment in *Fathers and Sons*. The expository and publicist literature of the time gives us partisan and partial views of what was happening. Turgenev gives us an objective view of what was happening. He does more than give us a variety of positions in an ideological struggle: he makes us feel what is going on and expresses too what is going on without the participants being aware of it. In broad outline he captures a moment when patriarchal Russia is under siege and in the process of change.

Turgenev's portrait of Russian patriarchal life is not idealized but one in which the strains and fissures of a way of life are visible. Pavel Kirsanov may be an inflexible representative of tradition and aristocratic privilege, but we sense that he too is responsive to the new currents swirling about him. This is shown by his emotion toward Bazarov and by his interest in Bazarov's work. And nowhere is the threat to patriarchal Russia shown better than in the portrait of Anna Odintsova, who has to make all kinds of sacrifices to retain some modicum of aristocratic privilege. Nikolay Kirsanov as well is beset by the changes in his relationship with the peasants and the new conditions that the imminent emancipation will bring to estate management. Turgenev is able to capture the tone and ways of aristocratic Russia, even while it is being subtly undermined. Beneath the novel's gentle and unruffled surface the currents of history continue to churn.

While giving us a superb historical novel, Turgenev has been able, somehow, to raise the issues to a universal level. We can read this novel without knowing anything about the 1860s in Russia. Many of the issues touch us today much as they did the readers of Turgenev's time. Complications of social structure, class privilege, the image of man and his vision—not to mention friendship, love, family, tradition, and the conflict of fathers and children—are all very much with us today, and Turgenev makes us feel their relevance then and now and probably always. No author in Russia or the West was able to assemble such burning ideological and personal issues and to show their interconnection and universality quite in the way Turgenev has with *Fathers and Sons.*

3

Critical Reception

Turgenev gives us a retrospective account of how he came to write *Fathers and Sons* in the 1869 article "A Propos *Fathers and Sons*."[3] Turgenev wrote that he was on the Isle of Wight in Britain in August 1860 when he first conceived of the idea for the novel: a young provincial doctor who made a strong impression on him there became the prototype for Bazarov. Turgenev had seen in the provincial doctor the nascent fermentation of what was to be called "nihilism." He was in Turgenev's view a new type that had appeared on the social scene but had not been perceived as such by others. In fact, there was no account in Russian literature of this new social type. The genesis of *Fathers and Sons* followed closely the ruling criteria in Russian criticism at the time: that literature catches and expresses the emerging social types of the period, and that it does this before others perceive the type. Nikolay Dobrolyubov in *What Is Oblomovism?* (1859) had spoken of the special sensitivity of the writer to catch the "scent" of the future.[4] The type exists empirically before the writer raises it to social consciousness by his work.

Most of the young generation of radical social activists and literary critics were outraged by the portrait of their generation in Bazarov.

They felt that Turgenev had delivered a calumny on their generation. Bazarov was crude, insensitive, and lacking in ideals, according to his critics. In "A Propos of *Fathers and Sons*" Turgenev writes, "The impressions I received at that time, although they differed in kind, were uniformly depressing. I noted an iciness, bordering on indignation, on the part of many friends whom I had found sympathetic and who had been close to me" (170). The file of responses to the novel that Turgenev accumulated includes the following: " 'Neither Fathers Nor Children,' a certain witty lady told me after having read the book, 'there's the real title of your novel—and you yourself are a nihilist' " (172). Another person wrote to him, "You are crawling at the feet of Bazarov"; and another, "You are merely pretending to condemn him; in reality you are fawning upon him and are hoping for a single condescending smile of his as if it were alms!" (172).

Turgenev was baffled by the critics, and nothing we know about him would suggest that he set out to insult this generation. Many important radicals and liberals, however, condemned the portrait. Alexander Herzen, for example, wrote in a letter of 9 April 1862, "You became very angry at Bazarov and out of vexation lampooned him, made him say all kinds of stupidities, wanted to finish him off 'with lead'—finished him off with typhus" (187–88). Turgenev replied, "In creating Bazarov, I was not only not angry with him, but felt an attraction, a sort of disease toward him, so that Katkov was at first horrified and saw in him the apotheosis of *The Contemporary*" (187–88).

Even more baffling for Turgenev was that he pleased the conservatives as little as the radicals. The conservative critics thought he had praised Bazarov and, as Katkov said, placed him on a pedestal. As a matter of fact, Turgenev's precise attitude toward his creation has been a matter of considerable dispute. While Turgenev was writing the novel his fellow writer P. V. Annenkov read it in manuscript. About Turgenev's relationship to Bazarov he wrote in a letter of 26 September 1861, "There are different opinions about him as a result of a single cause: the author himself is somewhat constrained about him and doesn't know what to consider him—a productive force in the future or a stinking abscess of an empty culture, of which one should rid oneself quickly. Bazarov cannot be both things at the same time, yet the author's indecisiveness sways the reader's thoughts from one pole to the other" (177).

In a letter to K. K. Sluchevsky on 14 April 1862, shortly after the appearance of *Fathers and Sons*, Turgenev was forthright in saying that he was on Bazarov's side: "I wanted to make him a tragic figure—there was no room for sentimentalities. He is honest, truthful and a democrat to his very fingertips" (185). And, "If the reader will come to *dislike* Bazarov with all his coarseness, heartlessness, pitiless harshness and brusqueness—if the reader should come to dislike him, I repeat, it is I who am at fault and I have failed to attain my goal" (185). Yet he also said to Afanasi Fet (an important Russian poet and close friend of Turgenev and Tolstoy) on 6 [18] April 1862, "Did I want to abuse Bazarov or to extol him? I do not know that myself, since I don't know whether I love him or hate him!" (184).

It is hard to know what to make of Turgenev's different comments. Alexander Herzen caught perhaps accurately the dilemma of Turgenev when he said, "The fates of the fathers and sons are strange! Clearly, Turgenev did not introduce Bazarov to pat him on the head; it is also clear that he had wanted to do something for the benefit of the fathers. But juxtaposed to such pitiful and insignificant fathers as the Kirsanovs, the stern Bazarov captivated Turgenev and, instead of spanking the son, he flogged the fathers. This is why it happened that a portion of the younger generation recognized itself in Bazarov. But we do not recognize ourselves at all in the Kirsanovs."[5] It would seem that Turgenev genuinely wanted to please the radicals, and he thought he had created a positive hero. His avowed political opinions would have placed him, too, on Bazarov's side. On the other hand, the novel shows Turgenev to be far more conservative in his social views than he admitted in public.

Some of Turgenev's contemporaries accepted the portrait as true and real. Many of these were conservatives who had axes to grind. N. N. Strakhov, a distinguished conservative critic and close friend of both Tolstoy and Dostoyevski, approved wholeheartedly and virtually without qualification of Bazarov and of *Fathers and Sons*. He saw correctly, I believe, that Turgenev's novel is set beyond the particular historical quarrel of generations, addressing itself to the conflict of all generations, and that the portrait of Bazarov is set against such eternal verities as nature, love, family, and friendship.[6] Strakhov went on to say, "He [Turgenev] clothed that mind [Bazarov's] with flesh and blood, and fulfilled the task with amazing mastery. Bazarov emerged as a simple man, free of all affectation, and at the same time firm and powerful in soul and body." As to whether the novel was written to praise or condemn the radicals, Strakhov confronted the issue squarely: "In short, is the novel written for the young generation or against it? Is it progressive or reactionary?" He evades a direct answer, however, for he ends up saying that Turgenev had written the novel for all possible audiences and that the conflict of generations was not limited to Bazarov's generation.

Alexander Herzen, the great populist and liberal of the first generation, had little good to say about Bazarov and records how negatively Dmitri Pisarev's contemporaries met his acceptance of Bazarov: "Pisarev's adversaries were frightened by his impudence, they repudiated Turgenev's Bazarov as a caricature and even more vehemently rejected his transfigured double; they were displeased that Pisarev had made a fool of himself, but this does not mean that he had misunderstood Bazarov" (232).

Of the important radical critics only Dmitri Pisarev recognized himself in the portrait of Bazarov and boldly accepted him as a correct depiction of his generation and a legitimate hero. He said, more or less, "Yes, this is the image of the younger generation and of me, and I am proud of it." He saw Bazarov as superior to every character in the novel in character, idea, and vision and justified every failing that others saw. He did not mean by this that Turgenev was correct in every detail, since Turgenev, according to him, had some axes to grind and could not help, by his own limitation, to distort the social portrait. Pisarev said that the younger generation could recognize itself in the novel's mirror, however clouded. He called Bazarov a "pure empiricist"—that is, "As an empiricist, Bazarov acknowledges only what can be felt with the hands, seen with the eyes, tasted by the tongue, in a word, only what can be examined with one of the five senses."[7] Despite this empiricist mentality, Pisarev goes on, Bazarov does not steal, does not beg for money from his parents, works hard, and wants to do something useful in life. What keeps him, guided as he is by instinct and self-interest, from committing evil deeds and what motivates him to do useful things? Bazarov does not, Pisarev goes on, commit evil deeds for the same reason that an individual will not eat a bad piece of meat.

Pisarev's point here is that in our moral decisions we are guided less by moral abstractions than by a kind of enlightened self-interest. We do not purposely hurt ourselves—at least an intelligent and clear-thinking person like Bazarov does not hurt himself. He works hard, studies, and lives decently with people because it is to his interest to do so. Although Pisarev does not mention Chernyshevsky in this article, it is clear that he is applying the latter's theories outlined in "The Anthropological Principle in Philosophy" (1860) and in his famous novel *What Is to Be Done?* (1863), wherein he describes a new vision of man, guided by enlightened self-interest, and in large part similar in attitude and action to the principles of Pisarev's defense of Bazarov.

CONTEMPORARY CRITICISM

Twentieth-century criticism of *Fathers and Sons* has directed its attention beyond ideological matters to the novel's structural properties; it views the ideological battles of the 1860s and 1870s in Russia under a universal gaze. In his 1983 study of *Fathers and Sons* David Lowe makes a case for the novel as a comedy.[8] He uses this term in the structural sense of a work that moves from complexity to simplicity and has a "happy" or harmonious ending. He leans heavily on Northrop Frye's conception of structure and genre for his interpretation. Matters of substantial importance, however, continue to be in dispute: the character of Odintsova, the duel between Pavel and Bazarov over Fenechka, the change that Bazarov undergoes between the beginning of the novel and its later chapters, and the love affair between Odintsova and Bazarov. Almost everyone sees Bazarov as a representative of the radicals of the 1850s and 1860s and specifically a representative of the views of Chernyshevsky and Dobrolyubov.

The identification of Bazarov with these two has not always been so firmly fixed. Victor Ripp, however, has widened the representation by making Bazarov a representative not only of the radicals but also of the liberals.[9] According to Ripp, Bazarov should be viewed as a representative of all progressive truth, not just the radical truth. Ripp sees Bazarov as representing the Russian *obshchestvo* (society), a term he uses for all those who sought a moral alternative to the status quo. There is something to this view, but it also blurs the novel's distinction between the radicals and the liberals. Pavel, to be sure, is not much of a liberal, since he clings to aristocratic privileges. But Nikolay Kirsanov and his son Arkady are open to change in an evolutionary sense, and in Ripp's interpretation it would be difficult to distinguish between them and Bazarov.

Anna Odintsova has drawn the fire of most recent critics. The words about her have been so unrelievedly harsh and so unfair that Annenkov was probably right when he read the novel in manuscript and wrote Turgenev, "My second remark concerns the splendid Anna Sergeyevna. That type is drawn so delicately by you that its future judges will hardly be able to understand it completely."[10] Isaiah Berlin calls her a "cold, clever, well-born society beauty;"[11] René Wellek characterizes her as "elegant, frigid, landowning widow Mme Odintsov."[12] And the Russian critic P. G. Pustovojt calls her a "cold epicurean."[13] The most recent studies continue this battering of Anna Odintsova. Joel Blair speaks of her emotions as dead;[14] Eva Kagan-Kans says that "though she brings destruction to Bazarov, she herself is untouched by any emotion; she is still lying under a blanket of snow and will always remain so."[15] It is interesting to note that Kagan-Kans blames Odintsova for Bazarov's destruction. I myself have defended Odintsova and pointed to her gentility, fairness, and reserves of character.[16] Her "coldness" I see as the caution she necessarily has after having been "abandoned" by her father in death with a ruined fortune and a sister to bring up and educate. It is such circumstances that lead her to marry someone she does not love; she is acting not from cynicism or cold-hearted calculation but from a sense of realism and duty.

The criticism of Anna Odintsova is in line with the almost unrelieved defense of Bazarov in his relations with her. Bazarov can do no wrong, and Odintsova can do no right. Edward Garnett speaks of Bazarov in rhapsodic terms: "Bazarov stands for Humanity awakened from century-old superstitions and the long dragging oppressive dream of tradition. Naked he stands, under a deaf, indifferent, sky, but he feels and knows that he has the strong brown earth beneath his feet."[17] Subsequent twentieth-century opinion has not materially altered this view of Bazarov. Critics still seem to excuse him everything—even his animal lunge at Odintsova has been excused as an example of his virility and vitality. Richard Freeborn sees Bazarov as coming out successfully in his relations with Odintsova because "Odintsova is almost as passive a participant in the relationship as was Insarov in *On the Eve*."[18]

Despite the stark contrast of the Bazarov of the first part of the novel and the Bazarov in the last part (after the failed love affair with Odintsova), many distinguished critics do not see any diminution in Bazarov's "tragic stature." Isaiah Berlin says that "Bazarov falls because he is broken by fate, not through failure of will or intellect" (Berlin, 29). It is difficult to know what is meant by "fate" and if such a concept would have relevance to a hero who believes in reason and will as the only agents of change. Only the Russian critic Pustovojt has the acumen and courage to point to what should have been obvious—that Bazarov undergoes an astonishing and troubling change during the course of the novel: "Up to chapter 14, in which Bazarov makes the acquaintance of Odintsova, that is, where Bazarov's basic plot is formed, Bazarov is a sober and intelligent person, who believes in himself and what he is doing and who is free of skepticism, pessimism; he is proud, sure of his goals and capable not only of influencing others, but of overpowering them with his knowledge, logic and will" (Pustovojt, 177). But after the change he is the opposite: "The hero does not succeed in remaining what he was before he met Odintsova. The wound is deep and he remains in despair to the end of the novel" (177). And to the end Bazarov cannot overcome in himself "feelings of spite, spiritual bankruptcy, irritation, and despair" (177). Pustovojt continues with a question that contemporary criticism is still trying to solve: "Where do such pessimism, skepticism, such joylessness and lack of perspective in the hero's views come from?" (177).

I have argued that Bazarov's fall from self-confidence to terrible self-doubt has been caused by his failed love of Odintsova. The love affair with Odintsova has compelled Bazarov to acknowledge forces within himself that override his will and his judgment. Bazarov had wanted to wipe the slate clean of authorities, but for Turgenev the slate is never clean. There are always natural authorities: love, death, birth, and the condition of man as something of an accident in an indifferent cosmos. This would seem to indicate that Odintsova helps reveal, but not cause, a weakness in Bazarov's makeup: the arrogance of his belief that he and enlightened men are masters of their own fate is the fateful weakness. This further indicates that Turgenev is positing that there are forces beyond man's ability to understand and use them (Wasiolek, 45). A. V. Knowles, however, disagrees with this view: "It seems farfetched to suggest that Turgenev has given him some innate death wish, or that his death is a form of suicide following Odintsova's rejection of his love."[19] Knowles suggests that the only hint supporting such suicide lies in Bazarov's pessimism about the future of Russia. It may be that Odintsova's role in revealing the fundamental spiritual weakness of Bazarov has led a generation of critics to demean and belittle her. Contemporary critics have even questioned her motives in coming to Bazarov's deathbed and have taken delight in pointing out that she keeps her gloves on so as not to be infected by Bazarov's cholera.

There has been, in short, very little negative criticism in recent Western studies of Bazarov and a determined effort to preserve his strength, truth, and firmness of will. Nowhere is this more evident than in the judgment of his death. Critics have almost without exception praised Bazarov in his dying, and probably deservedly so, since he dies with a stoic acceptance of his fate and neither pities himself nor blames others. Most contemporary critics would agree with what Strakhov said in the nineteenth century: "Bazarov dies altogether the hero and his death creates a shattering impression. To the very end, to the last flash of conscience, he does not betray himself by a single word nor by a single sign of cowardice. He is broken, but not conquered" (218–19).

Since Strakhov the praise for the dying Bazarov has been, except for a few cases, uniform. Freeborn, for example, speaks of Bazarov's death as "tragic grandeur" (Freeborn, 74). Wellek sees the death as a logical outcome of the defeats that Bazarov suffers throughout the novel: "His accidental death is the necessary and logical conclusion: Bazarov, the man of reason, the man of hope, is defeated throughout the book" (Wellek, 260). Ripp, however, says, "Even Bazarov's death, as Turgenev depicts it, is not so much a biological event as an illustration of how even this ultimate act loses all meaning for a man lacking any abiding confidence in who he is" (Ripp, 200). And Ralph Matlaw has questioned the "tragic grandeur" of Bazarov's death: "The end with Bazarov's disquisition on strength, life, and necessity strikes the reader as rather mawkish and hollow, for the words now have if not a false, at least a commonplace ring."[20] This may be a little harsh, and Knowles's reservation may catch a more gentle truth about his death: "His futile death underscores the relative insignificance of his philosophy and the transience of social problems" (Knowles, 80).

We can give Bazarov his beautiful and eloquent death and still fault his stand and vision, and it seems that Turgenev is doing that precisely. Bazarov and his real-life prototypes have made too great a claim for reason and will, and his arrogance is humbled by forces greater than he and mankind. Wellek seems to be concurring on this point when he says, "The book goes beyond the temporal issues and enacts a far greater drama: man's deliverance to fate and chance, the defeat of man's calculating reason by the greater powers of love, honor, and death" (Wellek, 659). Wellek's words echo what Strakhov said a century earlier.

There is little disagreement among contemporary critics as to the importance of Turgenev's art. Most of his contemporaries were unable to separate art from ideology; Dmitri Pisarev, however, was able to accept Bazarov as an accurate representative of the radical hero, and also a master of his art. He spoke of Turgenev's uncanny ability to represent objectively social types while letting them pass through his own prejudices and predilections. At first blush this would seem to be a contradiction, since Pisarev is praising him for being simultaneously objective and subjective. Pisarev has in mind that no one can be absolutely objective: one's personality always colors one's perception, but one can let that "colored" subjectivity remain what it is, or one can actively interfere with that objective subjectivity.

Pisarev's analysis is very acute and much more accurate than Freeborn's assessment of Turgenev's objectivity: "The objectivity of the work is remarkable on two counts. Firstly, in portraying Bazarov

Turgenev has achieved a masterly portrait of a type—the type of the 'new man'—with whose political and social views he was manifestly out of sympathy. Secondly, the novel possesses an organic unity, in which there are no narrative devices that obtrude into the fiction to distort, however slightly, the final impression of naturalness" (Freeborn, 72). (The second point is clearly an exaggeration and may be excused as coming from a diffuse praise for the novel's quality.) Many narrative devices obtrude into the fiction. The narrative, for example, is suspended early in the novel to give us in expository form Pavel Kirsanov's background and history. Such capsule histories suspend the novel a number of times, and though they are intrusive, we tend to accept them as a kind of artless convention.

One can question, also, whether the duel between Pavel and Bazarov follows necessarily from previous events. It strikes one as contrived and artificial. Freeborn again will permit no criticism of the novel. He says of this duel, "Yet the fact that they fight the duel ostensibly over Fenechka, the peasant girl, shows the way in which the ideological issues are welded into the structure of the novel. For Bazarov's readiness to fight the duel must be understood in the light of the fact that he is prepared not only to reject the *dvoryanstvo* [gentry], but also to devote his life in working for the peasants" (Freeborn, 72). Gary Jahn sees the duel more accurately: "Bazarov's participation in the duel is in itself exceedingly strange. With his initially consistent rejection of what he terms 'romanticism' nothing could be more surprising than his agreeing to submit himself to that epitome of the romantic, the code of the duel."[21] Ripp, however, excuses Bazarov's flirtation with Fenechka as "only an innocent exuberance in the presence of fresh beauty" (Ripp, 197); Knowles speaks of Bazarov's kissing Fenechka as "ignoble" (Knowles, 80).

If we try, with the advantages of 100 years of criticism, to answer the question so fought over by Turgenev's contemporaries—on whose side was Turgenev—we find that the question has not been settled in Russia or the West nor between nineteenth-century critics and those of the twentieth. We see Turgenev's situation in Russia better today than it was possible for him or his contemporaries to see it at the time. Turgenev was by nature not given to ideology; he was, in Henry

James's phrase, "the novelist's novelist"—someone by nature concerned with the formal and esthetic sides of writing.[22] As such he was unwillingly drawn into the ideological maelstrom of the time, and he tried mightily to please the radical critics. Most critics today still accept Turgenev at his word that he loved Bazarov and sympathized with his radical platform, but some have dissociated Turgenev from his willed identification. A. T. Lloyd is probably right when he says, "For all his admiration of Bazarov, Turgenev is too instinctively alien from him."[23]

The fact of the matter is that Turgenev loved Bazarov in conception, but the novel shows us that Turgenev had strong reservations about Bazarov. Turgenev's conservative aristocratic background shows through. The novel ends on a very conservative note, even though it is manifestly about a radical movement. The radical hero is humbled by natural forces—those of love and death—and the conservative family of the Kirsanovs—Nikolay and Arkady—continues the organic life of Russia, in work, love, family. Ripp points out the importance of family for Turgenev in this novel: Bazarov, Pavel, and Odintsova all fail to create a family, whereas Nikolay and Arkady celebrate the continuation of the family. Ripp sees this as a conservative or even regressive impulse in Turgenev, who apparently had no sympathy for the radical criticism of the conventional family. In *What Is to Be Done?*, by contrast, Chernyshevsky explores social relationships beyond the family.

In conclusion, we can say that contemporary critics continue to be impressed by *Fathers and Sons* and that the novel's account of specific historical events has not been an impediment to the general reader. We are more concerned today with the universal situations and relationships that the novel catches superbly. The generations then and now remain in conflict; the economic and social situations of different classes continue to change with historical events; man is still unsure about how much of life is under the control of his will and reason and how much is outside his control. The changing nature of family and love relationships is today, if anything, more rapid and problematic. Turgenev's magnificent sensibility caught all these in a way that is as relevant today as it was 130 years ago.

4

Turgenev's Worldview

Turgenev made his entrance on the literary scene in Russia with a series of sketches about peasant life, which appeared in journal form between 1847 and 1851 and subsequently in book form under the title *Notes of a Hunter* or *A Sportsman's Sketches*. Czar Alexander II was reputed to have been so moved by the sketches and the humanity with which Turgenev had painted peasant life that it prompted him to emancipate the peasants. True or not, this story shows that none of Russia's literati had seen and sketched the lives of the peasants with such sympathy and humanity.

The sketches are a series of pictures of peasant life painted by a hunter who wanders through the countryside and observes the peasants in their various affairs. In noting in detail and with accuracy the peasant life about him, he dignifies their lives by describing what had largely been ignored before then. Turgenev makes no effort to impose a special view on peasant life. The narrator-hunter is an objective observer, inserting himself into the narrative rarely. In "Bezhin Meadow," for instance, the narrator-hunter becomes lost at dusk after a day hunting and chances on a group of boys who are herding horses in the spring night. He spends the night at the fringes of their fire and listens, without verbal comment, to their talk. The boys talk largely about wood spirits and tales of the supernatural, and in the process they betray a whole range of human characteristics—liveliness, imagination, courage, fear, bravado, and concern for others. They are thoroughly humanized in the tale, and Turgenev and the narrator conjure up the variety and complexity of life by observing and describing it.

The narrator does not take notes indifferently; here and in the other tales he listens with sympathy, concern, and sometimes astonishment at the spectacle that unfolds about him. *Notes of a Hunter* may stand as a model for Turgenev's worldview and his artistic method: the ability to observe with precise detail and to suffuse those details with a lyrical sympathy. Turgenev is and will remain a "note-taker"—that is, someone taken with the circumstances about him, whether physical, psychological, or moral, and able to record them with accuracy and sympathy. He insisted that he did this in *Fathers and Sons*, and in "A Propos *Fathers and Sons*" he said that he treated ideological and political issues as he would items in nature: objectively and dispassionately. The outcry by his contemporaries as to whether he had described the social and political situation accurately is testimony to the fact that they all felt the grain of reality. But the difference of opinion was also testimony to the fact that the rendering of the social and political situation was not mere photography but involved a subjective element. Turgenev may have believed that he was describing the contemporary types as he would mushrooms, but in writing *Father and Sons* he betrayed distinct attitudes toward the types he had created.

Turgenev's views and values can be discerned in his fiction generally and in *Father and Sons*. He has a sense of what is good and evil, of what furthers humanity and what is destructive of it. In *Fathers and Sons* he disapproves of Kukshina and Sitnikov—that is, of ideological fashions, mindless imitation, and stereotyped thinking—and he disapproves of Pavel's inflexible adherence to form and tradition and of Bazarov's flirtation with Fenechka. There is a set of values or at least of discriminations in *Fathers and Sons* as well as in his other novels. By his objective and dispassionate manner we mean that the degree of intrusiveness in his creative world is small and that he does not actively intrude or distort what he "objectively" notes about his feelings.

Turgenev's contemporary Dmitri Pisarev made what is an important distinction about Turgenev's objective method. In the article "Bazarov" the critic Pisarev admitted that Turgenev was objective about the younger generation but was "subjectively" objective. By this Pisarev meant that Turgenev was not a clear sheet of glass through which the facts are seen but rather a sheet of glass that has been colored by Turgenev's personality. The facts are visible but slightly distorted by his subjective feelings and values but still objective in that Turgenev does not actively interfere with what is visible through the colored glass. What, then, is this set of values or worldview as it can be discerned in his creative works? What is it that Turgenev believed in, what purpose did he assign to man's endeavors, and where for him do happiness and fulfillment lie?

Readers of *Fathers and Sons* must calibrate the novel's ideological and generational structure with its structure of amatory pairing and the various failures and successes of both love and thinking. We would expect the "sons" to love differently from the way the fathers love—more realistically and rationally and free of the romantic aura they have projected onto women. Pavel again provides us with the best example of such traditional love, in which women are removed from real life and placed on a pedestal. His mysterious and unattainable Princess R. fatefully touches his life for all time. From the point of view of the sons, he "overestimates" the power of love and permits his life to be subject to its artificial power. The fact that he fights a duel over someone who reminds him of Princess R. is another item in his inflexible clinging to the romantic code and its special view of women. But one cannot conclude that all the gentry love in this way.

Nikolay does not love in this romantic and traditional way. He had loved deeply his first wife, but mostly as a companion, and his second "love" would seem to be one of gentle convenience. He marries one who is "near" rather than distant and one who is open and simple rather than mysterious and fateful. Arkady, too, does not love in the Pavel manner; nor does he love as Bazarov had initially advised—that is, practically and from physiological motives. There is some romanticism in his loving Katya, and some realistic and practical sense also. In one sense Arkady's marrying Katya is socially less adventurous than

Nikolay's marrying Fenechka. The father is more "radical" than the son, for Arkady makes a very conventional marriage: he marries someone of his own class and age.

Anna Odintsova, too, is of the gentry and despite her class and age marries no one for love; nor does she love fatefully and romantically as has Pavel. She marries her first husband for strictly pragmatic reasons and rejects Bazarov's advances for equally pragmatic reasons. She proceeds in her amatory relationships in a rational and realistic manner. Indeed, she seems to embody what Bazarov, and his real-life model, Chernyshevsky, would see as the "new" woman—self-reliant, pragmatic, and realistic. In this sense she is a challenge to Bazarov and Chernyshevsky's idea that the new woman must come from a new class and not from the gentry. What is lacking in her, however, from the radical point of view is some vision of social usefulness and good to which the new woman would dedicate herself. There is something of class rootlessness about her. In this period of historical change the aristocrats cope with the threat to their status and situation in different ways: Pavel with defiance and aggression; Nikolay with confusion; and Odintsova with curiosity and interest, but also with lack of purpose. Bazarov is the future for them, and he embodies in a forceful and aggressive way qualities they can see appearing in society.

Turgenev is magnificent in the way he catches the scent of changing Russian reality and the half-conscious way in which the gentry tries to adapt to change. Nikolay and Arkady seem to have change thrust on them and cannot remove themselves from changing circumstances as Pavel can. The novel is set in the years immediately before the emancipation of the serfs, and new arrangements of tilling the land are already part of Nikolay's reality. Nikolay does not cope well, and late in the novel when Bazarov and Arkady return to the Kirsanov estate we are given an avalanche of troubles that are besetting the poor Nikolay. Among these are hired hands asking for money, sloppy workmanship, the burning of buildings, the breakdown of machinery, and non-rent-paying peasants. Nikolay's problems do not occupy the foreground of the novel, which is taken up with Bazarov and his ideological battles with Pavel and his failed love for Odintsova. But as the main protagonists recede—Pavel to Europe, Bazarov by death, and

Odintsova into the cocoon of her leisurely habits—we become more and more aware of the concreteness and reality of Nikolay's struggles to cope with the changing conditions. Increasingly, too, Arkady involves himself with the work. Pavel does not work and lives in the past; Bazarov talks about work but with the progress of the novel works less and less.

If we are to make an analogy between the right ideological position and the right amatory relationship, then it would seem that only Nikolay and Arkady would fit such an analogy. They are the only ones who have successful loves. Indeed, Nikolay loves "rightly" twice. There is every indication that his first love was sincere and fruitful, and his love and marriage to Fenechka, though at first a matter of convenience, grows into a true love. So, too, is the love of Katya and Arkady. Arkady overlooks Katya at first, because of his foolish infatuation with Odintsova, but in the end he falls in love with her and marries her. It is not without significance that father and son marry on the same day.

If we look at the loves of all the other characters, we find that they are unsatisfactory or end in failure. Pavel's love for Princess R. ends in a lifetime of hurt for himself; Bazarov's failed love for Odintsova leads to his fateful change in life from bold confidence to despair and cynicism and finally to death. Odintsova marries, without love, for pragmatic reasons, cannot love Bazarov probably for equally pragmatic reasons, and in the end makes another "emotionless" marriage. Pavel, Odintsova, and Bazarov do not have children, and in that sense they lead barren lives. But if it is true that Nikolay and Arkady are right in love, is it also true that they are right in their view of life and how they lead it? That is, can we make a parallel between right loving and right thinking in their case? Or is Turgenev deliberately separating ideology and loving, or possibly putting them in contradiction? In view of the fact that the novel is structured on these two major themes—love and worldview—we cannot avoid bringing them into some kind of relationship.

It seems at first blush that Nikolay and Arkady cannot possibly represent right thinking, despite their fortuitous happy loves. Indeed, Arkady is given to stereotyped thinking and bears some resemblance to

Sitnikov in his slavish respect for Bazarov and his mouthing of radical clichés. But it is also true that as Bazarov begins to fall into cynicism about life, Arkady begins to separate himself from him in his thoughts and reactions. Still, if we are to make a connection between "right loving" and "right thinking," then Arkady would seem to present a considerable problem. No one, to my knowledge, has put him forth as a hero, and everyone would seem to agree that he is far inferior in character and thinking to Bazarov. Still, as Bazarov weakens as a hero, Arkady seems to gather strength. There is a growth to maturity in him. He shuffles off his youthful fascination with Bazarov and takes a more and more critical stance toward him, and he outgrows his infatuation with Anna and discovers a realistic and fruitful love for Katya.

Arkady is less intelligent than Bazarov, but he is also less given to harsh judgments toward others. If we set Arkady against Bazarov and Nikolay against Pavel, we see that both father and son meet life with more flexibility and acceptance. Neither possesses the hardness and inflexibility of attitude that we find in Bazarov and Pavel. It may be that their very uncertainty and mildness of judgment is what permits them to accept the realities of life and history. They are more open to life because they have judged it less. Nikolay and Arkady do not embody right loving and right thinking, only because Turgenev seems to be undermining the importance of the thinking. If we change these terms to *right loving* and *right living*, then Arkady and Nikolay would seem to embody them.

The father and son thrive not only in love but also in their work, whereas the other three lead barren lives. When Bazarov and Pavel fight their nonsensical love over Fenechka, Arkady is falling in love with Katya, and when Bazarov's life is coming to an end in bitterness and despair, Arkady and Nikolay are celebrating a double wedding and are deep in work on the estate. Turgenev seems deliberately to structure the lives of the various characters to favor that of father and son and to disfavor that of the other three. This is not to take away Bazarov's talent, strength of character, and vision, but it is to call into question something about his character and possibly something about his ideological program. The program and the man are in contradiction; the views he espouses in the first part of the novel envision man as in control of his destiny, ruled by will and reason, and capable of freeing himself from irrational forces. But Bazarov falls deeply in love with Odintsova—that is, he becomes captive of emotions despite his will. It may be that this impulse to control life, to bring the mystery and infinitude of life down to the dimensions of man, is what Turgenev is objecting to and what, according to him, strikes man's life as barren.

It is no accident that all three of our "barren" characters are highly disciplined and controlling characters. Pavel leads a disciplined life; he has not permitted anything new to intrude on it since his fateful love with Princess R. He is in "command" of his life. Although she is a much more attractive character, something of the same thing can be said about Anna Odintsova. She plans out every day, adheres to a strict schedule of activities, and wants to know the Latin names for all the plants. The "unknown" makes her uncomfortable. She rejects Bazarov because he is an unknown element in her life. She is in magnificent control of her emotions, which is to say that she is capable of rejecting emotions she cannot control.

Bazarov, to his credit, is less in control of his emotions than are Odintsova and Pavel, but this disposition brings him no pleasure. He wants to be in control and sees no profit in not being in control. He sees his emotional outburst at Odintsova as some sort of trick that nature has played on him. It provokes him to anger at himself and cynicism about mankind and its future. Odintsova and Pavel are at ease with their controlled vision of life, and because Bazarov is not, he is less at peace with himself than they. Bazarov has in many respects an attractive vision for mankind: man progressively eliminating "superstition," "irrationalities," and unquestioned truths in his life. But it is a vision based on man's progressive rational control of nature and society, and in holding such a view Bazarov can be charged not only with unreality but with enormous hubris.

Turgenev seems to favor Nikolay and Arkady precisely because they have no ideological vision or program and because they are incapable of the disciplined, rational control of Bazarov. Both father and son give themselves to the mysteries of love and children. Turgenev seems, also, to return to an "ideological" message in favoring Arkady and Nikolay, for what characterizes them is continuity rather than rupture. They are in a sense a traditional family but do not honor tradition in the barren and inflexible way Pavel does. Pavel does not work; Nikolay does, and finally so does Arkady. In the end the three "rationalists" are removed from the living currents of Russian life. Pavel has removed himself to Europe where he lives an idle and purposeless life, and Odintsova has married a foreigner. The double wedding in the second half of the novel is a celebration of continuity and of healing. By marrying Fenechka, Nikolay is breaching the peasant-master division and doing it by peaceful and fruitful means, in contrast to the radical stance of Bazarov; Arkady, in marrying Katya, signals a continuity within the younger generation of traditional values. Indeed, in the course of the novel the Kirsanovs—Arkady and Nikolay—represent a muting of the ideological and generational clashes.

In his letters Turgenev had spoken highly of Bazarov, specifically as a person on the threshold of the future. But the novel seems to deny what he was saying: it seems to pay homage to Bazarov's character, but it also criticizes, by implication, his program. The novel gives us a very conservative picture of life. Despite Turgenev's statement that he was in almost every respect on Bazarov's side, the picture that arises from the novel is a rejection of the radical program, an opting for traditional values of family and for gradual change, and most of all a reverence for the mystery and infinitude of life. It is clear, too, from Turgenev's biography and from his important 1860 essay "Hamlet and Don Quixote" that he believes in faith, imagination, and things unseen more than he does in reason and pragmatism. Because of the heated social climate when *Father and Sons* was published, Turgenev was led to put himself more forcefully on Bazarov's side than he would have in milder times. An examination of the content of *Fathers and Sons* and Turgenev's other novels shows us a worldview substantially at odds with some of the author's public comments.

5

"Hamlet and Don Quixote"

In the 1860 essay "Hamlet and Don Quixote" Turgenev divides humanity into "Hamlets" and "Don Quixotes"—that is, between those who are analytic, rational, self-reflective, and self-interested (the Hamlets), and those who are irrational, follow an ideal without reference to its consequences, and interested in something outside themselves (the Don Quixotes). This is a division between those who see the world as it is and those who see the world as they want it to be—between those who see a barber's basin as a barber's basin and those who see it as a magic helmet; those who see a fat and dirty peasant girl as she is and those who see her as a lady fair. In the final analysis the Hamlets stand for reason and analysis and the Don Quixotes for a faith in an ideal. It does not matter what the ideal is, but it does matter that one believes in something outside oneself. Turgenev expresses it this way:

> Don Quixote expresses in his person, above all things else, faith; the faith in something eternal and unchangeable, faith (in fact) in truth, the truth that is outside the individual, the truth that delivers itself to the individual on no easy terms, the truth that requires of him sacrifice and worship (in the knightly sense), the truth that makes itself his only after long warring and sovereign devotion.[24]

On the other hand, "Hamlet is, beyond all things else, analysis and egoism, skepticism personified. He lives only for himself."

Whatever the validity of such a division, what is important for our purposes is that Turgenev clearly puts himself on the side of the Don Quixotes, going so far as to say that when we stop having Don Quixotes in this world we might as well close the book on life. It is the Don Quixotes who are life-sustaining, not the Hamlets. Yet this is a surprising and astonishing admission on his part, because he is telling us that lack of realism, miscalculation, irrationality, and self-deception are what sustain life. Nor does it matter what we believe in, so long as we believe. We may mistake windmills for giants, a peasant girl for a lady fair, and barber basins for helmets; it does not matter that we are ridiculous, wrong, and ineffectual so long as we believe in an ideal outside ourselves. It does not matter that the ideal is false, as long as the belief in the ideal is there.

Turgenev tries to give Hamlet his due. Hamlet sees the world for what it is, and he suffers because of this. His skepticism does not prevent him from fighting injustice; he never falls into the errors that confound the Don Quixotes of the world. Hamlet types "are thoughtful and discriminating, persons of wide and profound understanding, but persons who are useless in the practical sense, inasmuch as their very gifts immobilize them." On the other hand, Don Quixotes are "useful to humanity and can set its feet marching because they see but one sole point on the horizon."

Turgenev's clear and unwavering advocacy of the Don Quixotes of this world would seem to imply that he has a profound skepticism of rationality, realism, and the objective world. Yet his fictional manner is devoted to scrupulous "note-taking" of the world about him. If we are to take the implications of "Hamlet and Don Quixote" as revelatory of what Turgenev believes in, then such realistic and objective note-taking would be an exercise in futility. If Turgenev is on the side of the Don Quixotes, then the world holds no objective meaning, only the meaning that we project onto it and a meaning of belief and not of fact. Faith, not reason, is the truth of the world. Those are right who ignore the "facts" of this world and follow the movement of their hearts in pursuit of an ideal. All of this is true, and Turgenev clearly favors the Don Quixotes, but the fact that he juxtaposes these two types would indicate that he is powerfully drawn to both, that he oscillates between the spirit of analysis and the spirit of faith, between a meaning that is objectively given and a meaning we create.

Turgenev is on the side of Don Quixote in his essay and perhaps in the deepest recesses of his being, but both impulses are to be found in *Fathers and Sons* and his other writings: the belief in the facts and the denial of the facts; the note-taking and the denial of the importance of the note-taking. Elena in *On the Eve* asks, "Why all this beauty, why this sweet feeling of hope, why this reassuring sense of some lasting refuge, of some safe stronghold, of some immortal guardianship? What then is the meaning of that smiling, beneficent sky, of this earth so happy and at its ease? Can all this be only what we feel within us—whereas outside, in reality, there is only an eternal icy stillness? Can it be that we are quite alone, alone—while beyond us everywhere there are only fathomless gulfs and chasms in which all is strange to us?"[25]

For Turgenev there are only fathomless gulfs and "eternal icy stillness," and this is why we must throw over those fathomless gulfs the veils of beauty, sentiment, love, and warmth. They will be found nowhere if we do not create them. The nature he lingers over in such loving detail and precision is the nature we see and cherish; the nature of cold and fathomless space and indifference is the nature that objective analysis gives us. Turgenev knows that if we give in to our Hamletian nature we will see only its "eternal icy stillness" and its brutal indifference to all our impulses for beauty and love. Turgenev's benign nature and his decorative social world were his quixotic defenses against a Hamletian despair. From Hamlet's point of view this benign nature and decorative and pleasant social world are deceptions, but from Don Quixote's point of view they are what the heart feels and wants, and for that reason they are real.

Turgenev never settled for himself which was real and which fantasy. Even if Hamlet, reason, and analysis are right and there is only "eternal icy stillness," we cannot and must not live with such a truth. This is what he means when he speaks of the quixotic impulse as life-giving. He seems to have anticipated Albert Camus's formulation in *The Plague* (1947) that we can act according to the brutalities of the universe or according to a human truth we create. It is conventional to speak of Turgenev's poetic realism—that is, his capacity to throw a veil of lyricism over the facts of existence—but the veils he throws are more than literary devices. They are underpinned by a worldview caught in the struggle he outlines in "Hamlet and Don Quixote." What beauty and love there is in the world is created by men and in the teeth of a brutal and indifferent universe. Turgenev is a gentle writer, and the cry of despair that issues from Elena in *On the Eve* is not characteristic of him. For the most part, he deals with the indifference and brutality of the universe by turning his back on it. This is why his literary universe resembles a garden, which is well-tended or badly groomed; why his dramas are played out in country houses, decorative salons, and what might appear to be artificial situations. But Hamlet and the vision of despair that Hamlet's vision raises is always fortunately shielded by the Quixotic vision that all will turn out for the best in the end.

In *Fathers and Sons* both principles are at work. Bazarov is surely a Hamlet in his dedication to reason, analysis, and science and in his rejection of the authorities of tradition, class, and unquestioned principles. He would surely have no tolerance for a Don Quixote who sees a princess in a fat peasant girl or a helmet for a barber's basin. A Don Quixote is someone who believes in a world unseen—in mystery and resonances beyond facts and measurements. And Bazarov will have nothing to do with mysteries. In his relentless rejection of everything that goes beyond his analytic control of life Bazarov is shown to be defeated by the very mysteries he rejects, especially the mystery of love. And like Shakespeare's Hamlet he deteriorates into skepticism, cynicism, and despair and finally seeks death.

There is no explicit Don Quixote in *Fathers and Sons*, but Turgenev gives the life-giving principle to forces that go beyond facts and the willed and rational control of life. He gives them to Nikolay and Arkady—to the love and marriage they celebrate, the children they bring into the world, and the work they do. This is not comparable to seeing giants in windmills, but it is living for something outside oneself and having faith in an ideal. Such faith may not be adequate to counter Bazarov's courage to look coldly into the depths of reality, and it may be a veil thrown across the "fathomless gulfs" of reality, but for Turgenev it is the best we can do and the right thing to do.

6

Turgenev, Chernyshevsky, and Dostoyevski

Fathers and Sons was at the center of a firestorm of controversy, and by and large—with the exception of Dmitri Pisarev—the radical establishment was not satisfied with the novel and especially with the hero Bazarov. To better understand the history of Turgenev's novel we can look at its relationship with two other classics of Russian literature: Chernyshevsky's *What Is to Be Done?* (1863) and Dostoyevski's *Notes from the Underground* (1864)—the former an answer to *Fathers and Sons* and the latter an answer to *What Is to Be Done?*

Chernyshevsky, the most important radical of the generation of the 1850s and 1860s, was the philosophical dean of the radicals and their most visible activist. If we are to understand the philosophical underpinnings of Turgenev's portrait of Bazarov, we must understand Chernyshevsky's view of man and society. He was very much on Turgenev's mind in writing *Fathers and Sons,* and most of Bazarov's views come directly from Chernyshevsky, with some important exceptions. Chernyshevsky came to considerable promise with the writing of his master's dissertation, "The Aesthetic Relations of Art to Reality" (1855). This treatise was an attack on the German idealistic conception of art, specifically Hegel's. German idealistic thinking on art had dominated many of the views of Vissarion Belinsky and others in the

1830s. In this sense Chernyshevsky was attacking his ideological fathers' view of art. This treatise outraged his philosophical fathers (he was denied his degree) and continues to outrage people today, both in Russia and in the West. The outrage comes from Chernyshevsky's dogged insistence on art as a reproduction of reality and denial to art of any "special" or "superior" reality. For Chernyshevsky, art is condemned to be inferior to reality. A copy is never better than the original, so that a real apple is better than a painted apple, and a real woman is always better than a painting of a woman.

These examples are particularly provocative, and Chernyshevsky used them for rhetorical purposes. Nevertheless, he is deadly serious in his argument. He denied any special reality or even special sensibility to art. Life, not art, was of prime importance, and whatever importance art possessed was derived from life. His contention that life was higher than art is in fact very much in the mainstream of Russian esthetic thought: Belinsky first announced the proposition that "life is higher than art." It is doubtful that Chernyshevsky would have provoked outrage only because of this proposition. Rather, it was his exploitation of the implications of this proposition and his literal and dogged application of it that led to the outrageous reactions. In this sense he is like Bazarov, who says extreme things in order to outrage his elders.

Chernyshevsky's belief that life was higher than art was consistent with his materialism and unidealistic stance in all matters. He understood that if life is higher than art, this does not mean that art is condemned to be a mechanical reproduction of reality. Near the end of this treatise he notes that art has an explanatory function, and as such it makes clear what is not clear to us in life. Such a function delivers art from "copying" life to "making" life in the sense that it brings into our consciousness what was not known before. It is precisely this function that is seized on by his disciple Nikolay Dobrolyubov when he elevates art to a pedagogical and even prophetic status, in the sense that the artist has a special sensitivity and perceives first what the average person has not been able to perceive.

Bazarov's aggressiveness toward art and his denigration thereof (a passable chemist is worth much more than a poet) comes directly from Chernyshevsky's comments in his 1855 essay "The Aesthetic

Relations of Art to Reality." Like Chernyshevsky, Bazarov is intent on aggressing against the unexamined views of the older generation, but there is reason to believe that he had nothing against a new kind of art. Both Bazarov and Chernyshevsky were arguing against a canonized and untouchable view of art—mystical, idealistic, impractical, and unquestioned. Both were arguing, too, against a view of the creative spirit that was too narrowly defined as pretty things said about love, nature, and mortality. In "The Aesthetic Relations of Art to Reality" Chernyshevsky argues at considerable length against a narrow definition of art—art confined to painting, poetry, and music. He argues that such things as jewelry-making and gardening are art also. While he attacks what is conventionally considered to be art, Chernyshevsky is at the same time arguing for an expanded conception of art, which would bring it closer to the everyday concerns of people. This is an argument Tolstoy will repeat in *What Is Art?* (1898). Turgenev seemed to have something of the same thing in mind when he spoke of the new poets of the age as "the American."

Like Chernyshevsky, Bazarov was a champion of science and its practical consequences for the betterment of men's lives. Both were materialists, and we can gain much understanding of Bazarov by understanding Chernyshevsky's concept of matter and human life. Chernyshevsky wrote what must be considered a blueprint of the radical view of nature in man—"The Anthropological Principle in Philosophy" (1860)—about the time that Turgenev was conceiving of *Fathers and Sons*. The keystone of Chernyshevsky's essay is a faith in the rational nature of man and the ability of science to understand not only the physical and material world but also the moral and psychological nature of man. Chernyshevsky gives us a quasi-scientific outline of man's place in nature, pointing out that nature is law-governed—that is, is a material phenomenon, and that material phenomena are governed by rational laws. We can understand by our reason and the set of procedures we call science the mineral and vegetable worlds, as well as the lower forms of life. But man too is part of material nature and is subject to the same laws that govern the other forms of material life. There is no difference, except complexity, between what goes on in the mineral, vegetable, animal, and human worlds.

Chernyshevsky believed in "the unity of the laws of nature," a phrase used to deny the existence of any idealistic superstrata—any second nature spiritual in character—above material nature. There is only one nature and only material laws. In the kind of optimism common in the nineteenth century, Chernyshevsky states that we have already learned the laws that govern the lower forms of life and that it follows that we will soon learn the laws that govern the highest forms of life. We are in the process of discovering the laws of man's body, and it will not be long before we discover the laws of his so-called psychological and spiritual life. We will soon learn the laws that govern how man feels, wills, and reasons. Once we do this we will be able to know how best to serve man's physical and spiritual needs. We will be able, in short, to create a better society—one that will serve man's real needs and not his imaginary needs.

In this soaring vision of man's future Chernyshevsky sees a man liberated from suffering and irrational and destructive impulses. According to him, the history of man's suffering has been largely self-inflicted in that he has misunderstood or has not been able to understand where his real needs lie. Man's real needs are material in nature—the most important of which is his self-interest. Hitherto man had misunderstood himself by denying his self-interest or by seeking his self-fulfillment in the wrong places. Man was not born to deny himself but to fulfill himself. He was not born for self-sacrifice and self-denial.

Chernyshevsky was attacking the more or less official doctrine of Western civilization that self-denial and self-sacrifice were good goals. He was aware that self-interestedness could be a destructive social force. But such hedonism was a misapplication of self-interest; it was the wrong kind of self-interest. Chernyshevsky believed that there was no contradiction between the right kind of self-interest and living for others. Indeed, he and his radical compatriots were intensely idealistic. What they wanted was a real self-sacrifice and a real idealism, not one based on hypocrisy and unrealistic self-denial. They did not believe in a self-sacrifice that denied oneself for the purpose of serving someone else but a self-sacrifice that was at the same time self-fulfillment.

Man cannot help being self-interested, but he can be stupidly self-interested or wisely self-interested. Stupid self-interest is what interferes with the self-interest of others, and wise self-interest is what furthers the self-interest of others. Stupid self-interest is pretty much what we would ordinarily call selfishness, envy, manipulation of others, domination of others, jealousy—the whole range of self-interested acts without regard to others or that hurt others. Wise or rational self-interest is the pursuit of ends that simultaneously satisfy one's self-interest and further the self-interest of others.

If one objects that such a mutually beneficial self-interest does not and cannot exist, Chernyshevsky insists that stupid self-interest has predominated because we have not been able to discern and formulate the laws of man's nature. Science, in other words, would rescue us from stupid self-interest. Once the laws of man's moral nature were discovered and formulated, then it would be possible to arrange the circumstances of man's life so that his self-interest would be fulfilled, working at the same time to satisfy his rational egoism and satisfy those of his fellow man. It will be possible, according to Chernyshevsky, to formulate what serves men's interest best and to arrange social conditions so as to fulfill this self-interest. Men will live according to these laws once they have understood them, for they will not want to live against their best self-interest. Man is destined, according to Chernyshevsky, to be happy and fulfilled. Pain, misery, and unhappiness are not in the order of things and have occurred in history because of ignorance of where man's true self-interest lies.

Chernyshevsky's view of "self-interest" outlined in "The Anthropological Principle in Philosophy" was dramatically portrayed three years later in his novel *What Is to Be Done?* Chernyshevsky was arrested in 1862 for his alleged subversive activities and certainly for his outspoken published views. He was to languish in prison until 1883, and owing to his uncompromising resistance to the czar he became the symbol of all radical and liberal sentiment of heroic resistance to autocratic repression. He wrote *What Is to Be Done?* while in prison awaiting trial. He had somehow persuaded the censors that his was an innocent domestic novel, and so it was published. The error was subsequently recognized by authorities; printing was halted, and an attempt was made to recall the copies distributed. All the copies could not be recalled, and the novel became enormously popular. It is probably the most influential novel ever written in Russia, for it served as a bible for generations of Russian revolutionaries. Its literary merit is another matter, since it is largely a didactic and philosophical novel.

What Is to Be Done? is a fictional rendering of the principles Chernyshevsky formulated in "The Anthropological Principle in Philosophy" and other philosophical writings. The novel gives us ideal characters who reject all irrational motives and who boldly work for a world in which man can follow his true interests. The characters are rational, hard-working, dedicated to the service of a better world, and self-sacrificing. When one of the heroes falls in love with his friend's wife, the husband does not fall into a rage or blame in any way his wife or his friend. There is none of the deception, misery, anger, and parade of destructive emotions that usually follow such a situation in literature and life. Rather, the husband sees rationally and analytically that the friend and his wife are better suited to each other, and he therefore abandons his claim to his wife, and the two men remain friends. Reason rather than irrational emotion governs his behavior. The novel celebrates the new men and women who, with the light of reason and enlightened self-interest, will bring to mankind happiness, harmony, and well-being. Bazarov resembles these characters in many respects, especially in his materialism, his lack of sentimentality, and his dedication to science, rationalism, and the rejection of established authority. But Chernyshevsky's characters are more idealistic and less sardonic than Bazarov, and they are not marred, as he becomes, by a failed love affair.

Chernyshevsky had Bazarov and *Fathers and Sons* in mind when he wrote *What Is to Be Done?*; his novel is in fact a corrective to *Fathers and Sons*. The reaction to *Fathers and Sons*, among the radical critics, was for the most part negative, and even someone like Pisarev, who accepted the portrait of Bazarov as a faithful representation of the radical generation, pointed out matters in Turgenev's novel that were at variance with radical beliefs. Pisarev and Turgenev distanced themselves from Bazarov's comments on art, but a bigger difference between the views of Bazarov and those of Chernyshevsky lies in the idealistic thrust of Chernyshevsky's beliefs. Chernyshevsky's heroes are unfailingly positive, and such positivism follows the premises of his philosophy of rational self-interest. Doubt, skepticism, disdain, cynicism, as well as misery and all destructive impulses simply have no place in the views of the new people and the new organization of mankind as envisioned by Chernyshevsky. Bazarov's caustic comments about others and his skepticism about life and its purpose are not part of the radical view of life, at least as Chernyshevsky and his followers conceived of it. The Bazarov of the second half of the novel—with his cynicism, despair, and death-seeking attitudes—is very much not a radical hero.

Chernyshevsky was aware of this, and he gives us as a corrective to Bazarov a genuine radical hero in the character Rakhmetov. Not an intellectual and harboring no sense of superiority over others, Rakhmetov is a man of the people, though mythic in stature. He sleeps on a bed of nails, eats only the coarsest of bread and does not drink wine. Contrast this to Bazarov's hearty appetite and his drinking of champagne at Kukshina's. Bazarov makes salacious remarks about women and sees them and love for them in physiological terms. Rakhmetov, on the other hand, has an ideal view of women and is chaste. When Rakhmetov saves a noblewoman's life from runaway horses she offers herself to him and he chastely rejects her offer. He is rational, sparing in appetite, and relentlessly idealistic. Women in the novel are not put on pedestals but are seen as working partners. Turgenev was well acquainted with Chernyshevsky's works. He admired him and dedicated a book to him. The deviations he painted in his portrait of Bazarov must be taken as deliberate. Since some of the traits Turgenev gives Bazarov are unflattering, we must assume that the author wanted to distance himself from the radical platform. We must assume, too, that he wanted to undercut the radical hero by identifying him with Bazarov and then giving Bazarov some undesirable traits.

As an answer and corrective to *Fathers and Sons, What Is to Be Done?* was itself answered by Dostoyevski's *Notes from the Underground*. These three works constitute an ideological battle of the early 1860s. Dostoyevski published *Notes from the Underground* in 1864—a work begun as a review of *What Is to Be Done?* The issues were so basic and important to Dostoyevski that *Notes from the Underground* went beyond a mere critique of *What Is to Be Done?* and became a philosophical testament. *Notes from the Underground* is a bitter attack on the philosophical principles embodied in *What Is to Be Done?* and by implication in *Fathers and Sons.* By way of the Underground Man, Dostoyevski attacks the principle that man can understand where his true interests lie.

Here Chernyshevsky's new world and new man are represented and bitterly satirized in the "Crystal Palace," a vision the Underground Man conjures up of the perfectly rational world, in which all of man's needs will be satisfied and where man will live in perfect happiness and harmony. This will occur because we will have arrived at what Chernyshevsky envisioned—a formulation of the laws of man's nature. We will know what his best nature is—not only his physical nature but also his moral and volitional nature. Once these laws are discovered, it is assumed that man will want to submit to them. All the laws will be comprehensive, and there will not be, nor can there be, any exception to them. To the extent that man does not live in accordance with them and rebels against them, he will live in a primitive and unenlightened state. Once he is enlightened he will live, of course, according to his best interests.

The Underground Man mounts a furious attack on this "rational organization of human happiness" in the name of "freedom" or, as he puts it, in the name of man's sweet caprice. According to the Underground Man, man will never submit to the Crystal Palace and to the perfect happiness it represents because the Crystal Palace leaves out the one interest that is more precious to man than happiness and harmony: freedom. Man, he goes on, will give up everything else to preserve his freedom. If it is asserted that man's freedom will also be formulated and the law of its nature discovered, and if it is really true that freedom itself will be rationally organized, then the Underground Man says that man will kill himself rather than submit to this rational organization of human happiness.

If *What Is to Be Done?* is a "positive" novel, then Dostoyevski's is a very "negative" novel. Dostoyevski seems to champion the value of pain against pleasure, irrationality against rationality, misery against happiness, complexity against simplicity, and destruction against harmony. He does so on the basis that the kind of vision Chernyshevsky pursues is humiliating and denigrating to mankind. Chernyshevsky's vision of mankind reduces man, as the Underground Man states it, to being an organ key on which the laws of nature play. The Crystal Palace, or the laws of nature, empty man of mystery, the future, time, development, and, in short, immortality. It is not that Dostoyevski champions pain and destruction in and of themselves, but for him pain and destruction are protests against the limitation of mankind and signs of man's mysterious and infinite nature.

Although Dostoyevski's attack on the rational organization of human happiness is directed specifically at the views of Chernyshevsky, it is also an attack on all socialist visions of man's destiny. Chernyshevsky was himself influenced deeply by European socialism and specifically by French utopian socialism; he is representative of a particularly aggressive and confident form of socialism. *Notes from the Underground* is a philosophical testament of Dostoyevski's rejection of socialism and all rational formulas for human life. In his subsequent great tragic novels Dostoyevski will continue to attack every form of socialist thinking. The attack is even broader than socialism; it is a rejection of every form of human pretension to definite knowledge about the nature of man and his destiny. In that sense it is a rejection of all forms of rational humanism, including the pretensions of science. Dostoyevski refuses to limit man by any conception of his nature, and he sees freedom as a guarantor of man's unlimited nature. Faith in God becomes a guarantor of that freedom, and for all practical purposes "God" becomes identical for Dostoyevski with man's infinite and immortal nature.

Turgenev's *Fathers and Sons* lies philosophically somewhere between *What Is to Be Done?* and *Notes from the Underground.* Bazarov comes across as less formulaic and more human than do Chernyshevsky's Rakhmetov and other characters in *What Is to Be Done?* Bazarov believes in reason and systematic science, in progress and the possibility of constructing rationally a better world. He has no use for mystery, superstition, and what escapes rational understanding.

On the other hand, the second half of the novel shows him to be deeply challenged by contradictions in his beliefs and deeply human in responding to those contradictions. To the extent that we can identify Turgenev with the total Bazarov—that is, the Bazarov of the first half and the changed Bazarov of the second half—then Turgenev, like Dostoyevski, reveals profound doubts about the reach of reason and its capacity to understand the most profound depths of human beings. Unlike Dostoyevski, however, there is no indication that Turgenev believes in some infinite and immortal nature of man, and certainly no evidence that he gives to God and faith the ultimate destiny of human beings. Nor in *Fathers and Sons* and his other novels does Turgenev accept pain, misery, and destruction as some kind of signs of man's essential nature.

Turgenev is a humanist but a tragic one. He does not have the faith—which he would consider naive—of Chernyshevsky that man can understand fully the nature of the world and formulate its laws; nor has he the faith that we can eventually build a world in which man will live in perfect harmony and happiness. Pain, destruction, misery, hate, and the whole gamut of negative emotions are part of man's nature and his world. Man looms large in Chernyshevsky's view of the world, and he looms large in Dostoyevski's view of the world. Indeed, in radically different ways both see man as dominant in the world.

For Turgenev, however, man is a small part of the world, and he has to learn to live as well as he can in a cosmos that dwarfs all of his pretensions to control his destiny. Man is born, lives, and dies without knowing why. If there are purposes, they are made arbitrarily by men and have no ultimate significance. In short, Turgenev's view of the world is much darker than Chernyshevsky's or Dostoyevski's. Despite the horrific world Dostoyevski created—in which the catalog of terrors that man has visited on himself and others is unmatched in the work of any other writer—he has a high view of man. He believes that man has an infinite and eternal nature, that spiritual joy and harmony are part of his destiny, and that a God exists to underwrite and guarantee these things.

Despite the ultimately dark view that Turgenev has of the world, there is no cynicism or despair in his world. Nature is shown by him to be beautiful and sometimes benign. Men are capable of beautiful acts, of love, dignity, sacrifice, and charity. They are also capable of cruelty, hate, aggression, and destruction. The mixture, for Turgenev, is part of man's world, and there is no promise that one set of qualities will predominate over the other. The best men can do is construct their own limited worlds and construct them with the most beauty and happiness.

Bazarov represents something of this view, but not all of it. He demonstrates considerable dignity in the face of death, and he has a firmness of character throughout most of the novel. But he makes too great a claim on the world, and he succumbs to too much despair when that claim is shown to be false. This is why Turgenev seems to cast his lot with those who live with a certain modesty and who accept the continuities of life: age, work, tradition, children, and death. But Turgenev has so constructed the world of this novel and of others that the tensions are never resolved. Arkady and his father, Nikolay, survive and flourish in *Fathers and Sons*, but one can read them, too, as creatures of habit who continue to do what others have done before them. Bazarov fails because he makes too great a claim on the world, but Turgenev gives considerable power and credence to that claim before it is destroyed by the faults in Bazarov's character and by death.

A READING

7

Structure

Fathers and Sons is not difficult to read: the cast of characters is not large, the plot is uncomplicated, and the moral and ideological issues are clear and well-defined. Indeed, Turgenev follows by and large the structure of his earlier novels. The master plot of his major novels is as follows: A young, well-educated visitor, with liberal and sometimes radical views, arrives at a manor house and engages in conversations, sometimes in arguments, with the inhabitants of the manor house. The inhabitants of the manor house often have some range of political opinion but are for the most part conservative. The discussions or arguments lead to tension, and the visitor leaves, usually under a cloud of some kind. There is usually a love affair contracted during the visit, which ends unsuccessfully. The visitor-hero usually dies at the end, and the essential position of most characters remains unchanged. The visitor's appearance is a troubling and discordant element in a society that is settled in its ways and conservative in its thinking. His departure (either in death or by going abroad) and the society's resumption of its old ways is a signal of the force of conservatism in the Russian gentry and of the radical hero's lack of influence.

Turgenev followed this general structure more or less in *Fathers and Sons* and the important novels that precede it: *Rudin, A Nest of*

Gentlefolk, and *On the Eve. Rudin* may serve as a paradigm for this structure. Rudin is an impoverished student and intellectual, no longer young, who arrives at a manor house, the society of which is fixed in its views and actions. He enchants the ladies and the young, turns the head of the daughter of the manor house, but fails to respond to her readiness for bold action. He leaves the house under a cloud because of both his thinking and his loving. Subsequently he is unable to find a home, neither economically nor ideologically. He dies on the barricades of revolution in France. Although there are satirical elements in Turgenev's description of Rudin, he is also shown to be sincere, fresh in heart, and endowed with the ability to draw others to himself.

The structure of *Fathers and Sons* is similar to that of *Rudin,* but the former and its chief character, Bazarov, are more complex and more powerfully rendered. Bazarov, who is young, well-educated, and radical in views, visits the house of the Kirsanovs, has a series of arguments with the conservative Pavel Kirsanov, and leaves the house under some tension and ill-feeling. He visits and falls in love with Anna Odintsova; the love affair is unsuccessful; he becomes disillusioned with life and dies. When the novel ends the essential relations in the Kirsanov household remain unchanged. Despite the power of his intellect and his character, Bazarov has no substantial effect on the people and conditions he encounters.

As with Turgenev's earlier novels, *Fathers and Sons* is built on ideological issues and love relationships. In it the amatory parings are an important part of the structure. Nikolay Kirsanov has lost a beloved wife, takes a peasant girl as his mistress, and has a child by her; in the end he marries her. Pavel Kirsanov has had an unsatisfactory relationship with a mysterious and eccentric Princess R.; the relationship changes his life drastically, and in romantic and mysterious way he continues to worship her memory. His subsequent life is a sterile sacrifice to her memory. Arkady falls in love with Katya, the sister of Odintsova, and marries her. Bazarov falls in love with Odintsova, and although she is attracted to him, she rejects him. Bazarov and Pavel fight a duel over the attentions Bazarov pays to Fenechka, the peasant mistress and future wife of Nikolay Kirsanov. There is also the enduring and peaceful love of Bazarov's parents for each other.

In *Fathers and Sons* and all of his major novels Turgenev conjoins ideological and amatory relationships. How one loves and how one thinks seem to be the two poles of his vision of mankind, and his heroes often show weakness in both areas. Turgenev the writer had a romantic admiration for the opposite sex, bordering on masochism. It would not be unfair to say that the women of his novels are stronger in character than the men.

Turgenev's art and technique tend to be "scenic," and the progress of a Turgenev novel resembles a play in that the novel consists of a series of settings or scenes, usually in a country house, where conversation takes place. The plots are simple and the movement proceeds by way of a series of static scenes, often in the form of visits to different country houses. It is of some interest that one of his earliest works was a play, *A Month in the Country*, and that he had a life-long interest in and admiration of the theater. The scenic structure is evident in *Fathers and Sons*, where Bazarov visits the Kirsanovs, then the country house of Odintsova, and then that of his parents. The novel is largely a series of visits and conversations: the incidents and scenes are not governed by necessity; there is no reason that we have just these scenes or these visits or these arguments and in that particular order. Incidents and acts do not move other acts, at least not in some necessary order. Bazarov's confrontations with Pavel Kirsanov could be fewer or greater in number; he could have visited Anna Odintsova once or three times and not necessarily the two times in the novel.

After Bazarov's visit to the Kirsanovs and his arguments with Pavel, there is nothing in those scenes to motivate his visit to Odintsova. The visit is presented as a chance visit, something decided on the spur of the moment and with no particular purpose. Indeed, Turgenev sets his actions in a context of random happenings, and there is an implied view of the world as something governed not by a particular logic but by chance and casual circumstance. On the other hand, Turgenev is intent on unfolding the views of various characters, especially Bazarov, and in giving us contexts that confer a probability and a believability on these characters. Character has a certain consistency, as well as mystery, from which action and drama proceed.

Although there is nothing ordained about who Rudin will visit and when he will leave, his character will repel by its excesses those it had initially charmed, and the abstractness of his thinking will prevent him from coping successfully with the concrete conditions he finds himself in. What seems to govern the fates of individuals and the direction of acts is the relationship between character and circumstances. Turgenev was very sensitive to the concrete political, social, and economic conditions of Russia, and his novels may be seen as interactions between these particular circumstances and the givens of different character traits. Bazarov's fate may very well have been quite different under different historical conditions, and different characters will have different fates under the same historical conditions.

Often the visits, conversations, and human happenings are set in the wider world of nature. The human scene is part of something larger—a world generally indifferent to what men do and say. Nature is often depicted as beautiful and benign, but still indifferent. There is a striking example of this in *Rudin*. The novel begins with the description of a magnificent summer morning: the fields glisten under a clear sky, a fragrant freshness comes from the woodland, and the sounds of birds can be heard. A young woman is seen from a distance walking on a country road between newly blossomed rye. This is Alexandra Pavlovna Lipin on a visit of mercy to a dying peasant woman. The scene is characteristic of Turgenev in that the human being and the action of the human being are placed in a natural context broader than the human drama. What dominates this opening scene is nature, and it is only gradually that human beings and their purposes come into focus. Even though the human drama concerns mercy and death, the natural context is indifferent to the human context. Many authors show nature to be cruel and harsh in its indifference to the pathos and longings of human beings. This is the way Turgenev shows nature to be in *On the Eve*, where the longings of love and life are callously disregarded by the natural world. For Turgenev, nature is always the larger context, and in its indifference it can be benign and beautiful as well as harsh and unforgiving.

Structure

Nature is less prominent in *Fathers and Sons* than in some of Turgenev's other novels, but it is no less dominant. Its presence seems to increase in the second half of the novel, where some of the pretensions of the human world are noted and deceived. In the first half of the novel the social issues that are raised by Bazarov and represent fairly accurately the intense social environment of that historical moment seem to make nature recede before purely human concerns. The radicals of the 1860s had the pretension—and it is one shared by Bazarov—that human will and reason can "correct" and direct nature. In the first half of the novel nature is represented as something used by human beings. Nikolay Kirsanov comments about forests and fields as he is driven back to the manor house with his son Arkady, but his comments are concerned with the economic status of these fields and forests. Bazarov roams through the fields in the early morning, but it is to gather, dissect, and study frogs. Nature is used for scientific purposes.

Only Nikolay and Arkady, at selected moments, are aware of nature in and of itself, but both are made to feel ashamed of such sentiments. Pavel is at odds with Bazarov in how one "directs" and uses nature, but not in the belief that man should do so. He lives in a thoroughly "social" world, formed by a set of inflexible social codes, and though he lives in the country he seems to have no feeling or awareness of nature. Odintsova, too, is comfortable with a nature that has been named, domesticated, and ordered by the human mind. Bazarov is initially thoroughly immersed in a human social consciousness, and he becomes aware only gradually that there are forces in nature that go against the grain of his reason and will.

Part of the overall structure of *Fathers and Sons*, then, is its being set in a thoroughly human and social environment (country houses, drawing rooms) and yet having this human and social setting placed in a broader natural setting that is shown to condition human action by laws that are inscrutable and perceived to be indifferent to human purpose. Turgenev is not pessimistic about the relationship between human purpose and nature: man is not rendered insignificant because of nature's power or indifference to his acts and consciousness, but he has to work out his limited meaning in harmony with nature's laws and presence.

Turgenev's strengths are not, as he cheerfully admitted on several occasions, in constructing plots or imagining situations. In "A Propos *Fathers and Sons*" he wrote, "I must confess that I never essayed to 'create an image' unless I took as my point of departure not an idea but some living person to whom suitable elements were gradually added and applied. Since I am not possessed of a great deal of untrammeled inventiveness I have always had need of some specific ground that would be firm underfoot" (169). On the other hand, he has a remarkable ability to create vivid characters even if they do very little that we would characterize as interesting and unusual. The characters come to life with their voices. We know who Bazarov is and what he stands for after he speaks for a few minutes, and the same is true of Pavel Kirsanov. Turgenev's touch is light, and he does not labor heavily to give us the inside of a character. When he feels that background information is needed, he gives it directly in a summary narrative form, as he does for the lives of the Kirsanov brothers and for Odintsova. These are almost always external facts about the lives and almost a chronology, however; he does not give us a lengthy analysis of the characters' inner lives. They reveal their essential selves by what they say and do.

In *Fathers and Sons* the characters' psychology is got at inferentially from the objective facts. We know that Pavel Kirsanov is an inflexible, highly disciplined, opinionated character, attached to the past and an enemy of change, from what he says, not from what Turgenev says about him. All this is particularly true of Bazarov, the novel's most complex and interesting character. We know almost nothing about him from Turgenev; we are told almost nothing about his background. He is what he shows himself to be, and there is still considerable controversy about who he is. Bazarov's character is not "emptied" and closed by narrative definition. Turgenev "shows" rather than "tells"—a Jamesian distinction, and surely one of the reasons that Henry James admired Turgenev's craft so highly.

Turgenev may appear to be old-fashioned in the directness of his manner and the ease with which he comments on his characters. But he is also very modern in the way he permits his characters to present themselves without his intrusive analysis. Both Hemingway and James looked to Turgenev as one of their masters, and both praised his art. Considering how substantially Hemingway and James differed in their craft, their common agreement on the skill of Turgenev points to the variety and complexity of his craft.

8

Art and Ideology

Despite their respect and admiration for Turgenev and their praise for his handling of nature, love, and human relations, neither James or Hemingway seemed aware of the Turgenev who was deeply embroiled in the politics of his generation. It was Turgenev's fate to live at a time when political and social questions were foremost in the minds of Russian intellectuals and when it was expected that a writer would address himself to those questions. The time in which Turgenev wrote *Fathers and Sons* was ideologically white-hot, and no writer in Russia, including Turgenev, could escape the demands of the times. His talent and proclivities were essentially poetic, but there was no way in which he could confine himself to literary matters alone and find a sympathetic readership in Russia. In the West we expect our writers to do their inventing at their ease or unease, often to do it alone and with the freedom to ignore social questions. Gustave Flaubert, who functions so much for us as the prototypal Western writer, had his historical rages, and surely his novels, especially *Madame Bovary*, contained significant social commentary, but no one would have thought of demanding that he write this or that. Yet the traditional role of the artist in Russia—in the nineteenth as well as the twentieth century—

demanded that the artist involve himself in and comment on the nation's current, pressing ideological and philosophical problems.

Russian literature was looked to as a moral and social guide, and the writer as a fount of truth. His task was to bear witness to the present and the future. The concept of the solitary writer singing to himself was repugnant to Russian critics and writers. Art for art's sake, which has something of sacrament for us in the West, was a repugnant doctrine—trivial, self-indulgent, and worthless—to Russia's influential critics of the 1850s and the 1860s. With very few exceptions the distaste for art for art's sake runs across the various ideological lines. Vissarion Belinsky, whom Turgenev deeply admired, said that "life is higher than art"—a proposition accepted without criticism by the public at large and by Russian writers. A work of art was to be judged, praised, or commended on what it said about society.

This social commentary, moreover, was to be not only an objective reflection of the current social circumstances: writers were expected to be engaged and to use literature as a means for the attainment of truth and as a guide to a better society. The reigning literary criteria called for the depiction in literature of social types—that is, distilled representations of types that existed in the empirical world. Such typology was supposed to make clear to the reader what was at work in the society. Even more, such typologies were forward-looking in that the artist's greater sensitivity allowed him by way of his "types" to discern what was in the offing, what was on the horizon of society's development. The artist was something of a "seer" in that he saw first what the average man was not able to make out. In addition, the artistic portrayal could and did act as "recommendatory"—that is, it had the weight of truth and took on a pedagogical or rhetorical function. The types were models to be imitated and their programs were to be worked for and implemented.

Turgenev responded, probably without reflection, to these demands. He wrote a number of novels in the 1850s, all constructed around a central character type in contemporary society. *Rudin* (1855) depicts a university student, poor and marginal in social standing, who visits an estate, astounds all the aristocratic characters with the power of his intellectual vision and his brilliant talk; he falls in love with the daughter of the lady of the manor, and when the young girl offers to run away with him, he falters, becomes frightened, and flees the offer. Rudin was Turgenev's version of a new Russian type: the rootless intellectual looking for a place in Russian society and seeking also to have some impact on it. The radical establishment found the type unsatisfactory and faulted Rudin for being a "talker" rather than a doer and for lacking firmness of will. The first time he is confronted with an action to be taken—accepting the offer of a young lady's love and her desire to run away with him—he turns tail and runs.

Turgenev was intimidated by the radical critics and tried again to satisfy their demands with *A Nest of Gentlefolk*, written a year later (1856). Here he chose to portray an aristocrat who searches for the truth and imbibes the rational thought of France's eighteenth century (Voltaire, Rousseau, etc.). Lavretsky wants to be of use to his society but is unable to find his place in either the city or the country, the past or the future. He is a failure in his amatory life, as was Rudin. First he marries an idle, faithless, and luxury-seeking beauty, and then he falls in love with a quiet, traditional Russian girl. Despite his efforts to live simply and honestly and to be of use to society, Lavretsky does not meet the the radical demand for a positive hero. The positive hero the radicals demanded was to be strong in will, rational, fearless, and dedicated to the obliteration of superstition, tradition, and privilege. Turgenev had caught in *A Nest of Gentlefolk* the type of the sincere aristocrat who attempts to cope with a changing world and does so with uncertainty and confusion. The criticism from the radical thinkers was merciless, and the beleaguered Turgenev tried a third time.

This time it would seem that he had succeeded in meeting their demands. In the novel *On the Eve* Turgenev drew a hero who was firm, active, positive, unswerving in the defense of his country, and ruthless before his enemies. But the hero turned out to be a Bulgarian, not a Russian, which brought even sharper attacks on Turgenev's attempts to satisfy the radical critics and fulfill his duty as a writer of his generation.

Finally, in 1862 he gave them Bazarov, a hero of strong will, a relentless antagonist of aristocrat privilege, dedicated to reason and progress. It would seem that the radical camp finally had its positive hero, and there seems little doubt that this is what Turgenev had consciously tried to provide. Bazarov is, after all, a foe of unthinking tradition, the status quo, and superstition and a fearless proponent of a life guided by reason, strong will, and honest analysis. But the novel and the portrait of Bazarov raised a firestorm of criticism. Almost without exception the radicals rejected the portrait as historically inaccurate; they felt insulted by it—by Bazarov's crudeness and roughness of manner and by his lack of ideals.

By his nature and sensibility, Turgenev was probably not drawn to the fierce ideological debates of his time, but there was no question of ignoring such debates. He addressed himself to such questions in the same way he depicted the world about him: by meticulous observation and objective rendering. All of his major novels, including *Fathers and Sons*, weave together very human and personal themes with ideological issues. In this sense Turgenev was able, with great skill, to bring together what is timely and timeless. The ideological debates hold the foreground in *Fathers and Sons*, but the debates take place against the background of such universal themes as love, death, family, and friendship. His contemporaries read *Fathers and Sons* as a representation of the ideological conflicts of the 1860s, but today we can read *Fathers and Sons* with little or no historical knowledge of the issues of the time.

Most novels tied to historical issues die with the passing of those issues. *Fathers and Sons* is at once of the times and above the times. Turgenev has managed to capture the issues and spirit of the times without binding his novel to the past. Such characters as Pavel Kirsanov and Bazarov occupy distinct political and ideological positions, but they are not mere mouthpieces for such ideas. It is difficult to imagine Bazarov apart from the political and social views that he holds, yet Bazarov is more than a spokesman for a political type. Turgenev has been able to meld character and idea in a living unity and believability. D. S. Mirsky may overstate a bit Turgenev's melding of art and politics, but he is by and large correct when he says, "*Fathers and Sons* is Turgenev's only novel where the social problem is distilled without residue into art, and leaves no bits of undigested journalism sticking out. Here the delicate and poetic narrative art of Turgenev reaches its perfection, and Bazarov is the only one of Turgenev's men who is worthy to stand by the side of his women."[26]

9

The Two Generations

In *Fathers and Sons* the most important clash between the generations takes place in the Kirsanov household between Pavel Kirsanov and Bazarov—between a representative of the "old" generation (the fathers) and one of the "new" generation (the sons). There are two fathers, Pavel and Nikolay, and two sons, Bazarov and Arkady. Bazarov and Pavel occupy the extreme positions of social conflict and Nikolay and Arkady a less contentious and more moderate opposition. The central figure and the center of interest, both ideological and dramatic, is Bazarov, and the progress of his person and his views constitutes the main line of development. One can argue that everything is more or less structured about Bazarov: that every other character throws some light on his person and every other view or position helps define better Bazarov's ideological position. The main structure of the novel, then, is to follow the progress of Bazarov's position as it comes into relationship with conflicting positions and the progress of his person as he comes into contact with other characters. This is a character-centered novel, and nothing happens to distract us from observing, analyzing, and understanding Bazarov.

Bazarov's ideological clash with Pavel Kirsanov is the most obvious conflict, and the conflict helps define early and clearly who

Bazarov is and what he stands for. Arkady is there in the early chapters to set off the intelligence, dedication, and seriousness of Bazarov's commitment to radical positions. Sitnikov and Kukshina are introduced later to set off something of the same thing and to remind us that Bazarov's ideas can be trivialized and cheapened by fashion and shallow thinking. Bazarov's relationship with Anna Odintsova serves as a test of his views of women and love and shows us and himself that he has been deeply wrong about himself. The relationship occurs in the middle of the novel and serves a kind of fulcrum for a decisive change that occurs in Bazarov's character. His relationship with his parents tells us something about his background and is an implied criticism of the view that circumstances automatically create character. Bazarov comes from a caring, loving, tender, and sensitive family, yet the most salient traits of his personality are revolt, skepticism, anger, rudeness, and confidence bordering on arrogance.

The novel begins with the elder Kirsanov, Nikolay, anxiously awaiting his son Arkady's return from the university. The house servant Peter, who is at Nikolay's side, is described as such: "his turquoise earring, and his hair (mottled and slicked down with pomatum), and the deferential wrigglings of his body—betrayed a man of the new perfected generation" (3). Peter has adopted some of the mannerisms of the gentry he serves, but he continues to cower before them, thus "the deferential wrigglings of his body." Immediately after these remarks Turgenev interrupts the scene with an exposition of some four pages in which he gives us a brief history of Nikolay's and his brother's background. It is astonishing how easily the reader accepts this interruption. There is an artlessness, or the appearance of such, in the direct and simple way in which Turgenev introduces the exposition. It is almost as if he says, "Well, while Nikolay and Peter are waiting for the return of the son, I might as well use the time to tell you something about Nikolay's background." There is also an implied contrast between past and future—a major theme in the novel—by way of the history of Nikolay and the impending arrival of the son and his future.

The background narration is interrupted by the arrival of Arkady. The "future" in the arrival of the two young men arouses Nikolay from his reverie and interrupts the summation of the past being given. The father covers his son with kisses, but Arkady's response is more restrained, and he distances himself from the emotion by pleading the need to shake off the dust from his clothes: "Do give me a chance to shake some of the dust off, Dad" and "I'll get you dirty" (8). The difference in response is partly that of a young man who feels himself grown up and who wishes to be treated with the emotional distance of adulthood, and partly the result of the views that Arkady has adopted under the influence of his friend Bazarov. It is no accident that the third sentence Arkady addresses to his father is an introduction of Bazarov: "Dad," he says, "allow me to introduce you to my friend Bazarov about whom I've written to you so many times. He has been kind enough to accept an invitation to stay with us" (8).

In a sense Arkady thrusts Bazarov between himself and his father's attentions, as indeed Bazarov will be a barrier between Arkady and his father and especially his uncle. What has occurred during Arkady's absence at school and the change that his father sees and somewhat fears is embodied in Bazarov and everything Bazarov represents. This is so on a personal level but also on the broader level of general change for Russia. Bazarov and everything he represents is the new and divisive element between the generations. Arkady has come home, but he has not come home as he left.

The beginning strikes the first note of one of the major themes: the "meeting" of old and new, of father and son, and of the strange and the familiar. Nikolay Kirsanov's peering into the distance is a kind of peering into the future and a kind of effort on the part of the older generation to discern what is coming (the future) in the younger generation. The new is Arkady, but more so his friend Bazarov, who for the older Kirsanovs, arrives unexpectedly. Bazarov is the new, strange, and unsettling element, and Arkady, his disciple, is the new but familiar element for the fathers. Arkady is a disciple and admirer of Bazarov, and his resistance to his father's emotionalism is our first example of what the new generation represents. Bazarov will stand for a dry, pragmatic, unemotional view of reality and the needs of the times. When Arkady introduces Bazarov to his father, Bazarov offers the father a red and gloveless hand, which he is "a little slow in extending" (9). When asked for his patronymic, he gives it in an "indolent voice" (9) and with no addition for courtesy's sake. Even when Nikolay says that he hopes Bazarov will not find it dull to be staying with them, Bazarov's "lips stirred the least trifle, but he said nothing" (9).

Bazarov disdains to match Nikolay's social grace and conventional greeting with one of his own. In this opening scene he hardly talks, and his manner in all things is one of austerity and spareess, which will match his essential pragmatic nature. Indeed, in this opening scene Bazarov speaks only a few words, gives his name to Nikolay when asked, commands the driver of the tarantass to get going, and then later interrupts Nikolay's quoting of Pushkin by asking for a light for his pipe. He will be a critic of verbal eloquence and indeed of useless words. The older generation "talks," and the younger generation—at least those of whom Bazarov is a representative—"does." The interruption of Nikolay's quoting of Pushkin is no accident, for by this act Bazarov shows his displeasure with poetic eloquence and his concern with practical matters. When they arrive at the manor house, Bazarov's first words, in response to Nikolay's saying that they must sup soon, are, "A bite wouldn't be at all a bad idea" (19).

The details of the first pages call our attention to an important element of what happens subsequently. The gloveless, reddened hand draws our attention to Bazarov's class status and to his view of work and leisure. Bazarov is of a different class from Arkady. His family is marginal gentry, and as a student he represents an undefined class. Indeed, he represents the rise of a new social class in Russia, the *raznochintsy*—"of varied class" or "in-between class." This in-between class originated in the 1820s with the rise of universities and was composed of university-trained students, sons of priests, and writers from outside the aristocracy. The *raznochintsy* were by and large responsible for the social unrest in the 1850s and 1860s; members were well-educated, landless for the most part, and faced with the prospect of careers as civil servants or in the military. Because the *raznochintsy* were for the most part liberal or radical and wanted social change in Russia, they found working for either the government or the military anathema. Many took up—as did Bazarov's historical prototypes, Chernyshevsky, Dobrolyubov, and Pisarev—literary careers and specifically the editing of important journals, which provided them with marginal economic support and with the means to propagate their views.

Bazarov, as a representative of this class, occupies an aggressive position against aristocratic privilege and stands for a democratic and proletarian relationship to work. His reddened hands will contrast with Pavel Kirsanov's immaculately groomed fingernails. Bazarov has a contempt for everything aristocratic. Arkady, on the other hand, is caught between the new values of his fellow student and the old values of his father. He loves his father, but he is eager to show that he is liberal in thought and deed. Arkady is in conflict between sincere old feelings and the overlay of the new views he has learned at the university and presumably from Bazarov. In this sense he is not of one piece, as is Bazarov. Bazarov, on the other hand, seems to be at home with himself and sure of his views.

Arkady has his father's good nature, but under Bazarov's influence he wants to demonstrate his independence from his father. His ambivalence is shown repeatedly. His father pats Arkady on the shoulder and knee to Arkady's discomfiture, and Arkady turns the conversation away from intimacy to practical details. On the other hand, he kisses his father spontaneously when he learns that his father had waited five hours for him. At one point, too, Arkady waxes eloquent about the fragrance of the air and the sky of the region, and then checks himself and looks over his shoulder at Bazarov, presumably from fear that he has violated some nihilist premise, both in showing so much emotion and in showing so much attachment to something as irrational as the land or the place of one's birth. When his father says that it is natural to be impressed by the region of one's birth, Arkady dismisses the importance of one's birthplace: "Come, Dad, it's all the same where a man happens to be born" (13).

There is a conflict in Arkady between what he feels and what he thinks. And it is what he thinks that here takes precedence, especially when he turns to look at Bazarov, either for confirmation or fear of disapproval. The radicals believed in rationalism and realism and were against all mysticism or special feelings. Attachment to the place of one's birth would be considered irrational and mystical. We know that Bazarov disapproves of excessive emotion and feels that man is not individualized by the specific circumstances of his birth and upbringing. He will later tell Odintsova that men are like trees in the forest and that a botanist does not bother to study each individual tree—that is, Bazarov in his program of beliefs disapproves of individualism.

Arkady and his father also discuss the running of the estate, and something of the economic circumstances of the estate and by extension in Russia at the time is communicated to us. Nikolay shows himself to be helpless in a deteriorating situation: the peasants are not paying rent; the hired hands are sabotaging his efforts, damaging his harnesses; and the land is by and large being worked ineffectively. The dissatisfaction and hostility of the peasants are signs not only of Nikolay's inability to handle the situation but also of the state of the relations between the gentry and the peasants.

Fathers and Sons was written right before the liberation of the peasants in 1862 and published immediately thereafter. Liberals had made the freeing of the serfs the highest priority for several decades, and the radicals, like Bazarov, arose in part from the social ferment and agitation for this great reform. The major confrontation between the aristocratic Pavel and the radical Bazarov occurs, then, in a period of change and most of the principal characters find themselves adjusting to that change. It is a time of uncertainty for both gentry and peasantry, and a changing power relationship generates uncertainty and hostility. Nikolay may be kind and soft-hearted, but he is capable of defending his class interests. During the trip home they pass a forest, and Nikolay tells Arkady that he has sold the forest. Arkady asks, "What made you sell it?" (15), and Nikolay answers, "I needed the money; besides that, the land is going to the *mouzhiks*" (15). Nikolay is not above stripping the land of most of its value before it becomes the property of the peasants. The class relations between gentry and peasants do not play a major role in the novel, but the relations are part of the atmosphere in which the class relationship between the gentry and Bazarov's new aggressive class are worked out. Turgenev captures very subtly and sensitively the fluid class relationships then part of the scene in Russia.

During the ride home Nikolay tells his son that a peasant girl is now living with him in the house. Arkady responds with a high-minded liberalism of indifference and soothes his father's anxieties, especially the anxiety that the guest Bazarov might find the arrangement embarrassing. We notice that in these opening scenes Arkady introduces Bazarov to his father and to us: our first impression of Bazarov is largely given by way of Arkady's view of him. This device has several structural functions: by distancing us from Bazarov, a certain mystery is introduced and with that mystery an expectation and eagerness to confront him directly. It also underscores the role Arkady will play in the first part of the novel—that of intermediary between the elder Kirsanovs and Bazarov, between the strange and the familiar.

10

Pavel and Bazarov

We meet Pavel Kirsanov, Arkady's uncle and Nikolay's brother, shortly after the three arrive at the manor house. His physical appearance stands in stark contrast with Bazarov's. Pavel is elegance itself, with his immaculately groomed fingernails, his snowy-white cuffs, and his exquisite manners: "He appeared to be forty-five or so; his closely clipped gray hair gave off a dark sheen, like minted silver; his face, jaundiced but unwrinkled, unusually regular in features and clean-cut, just as if it had been outlined by a fine and delicate graver, had traces of remarkable good looks" (20). And "Pavel Petrovich took his beautiful hand with long pink nails out of his trouser pocket, a hand which appeared still more beautiful because of the snowy whiteness of the cuff, linked with a large opal solitaire, and offered it to his nephew" (20). Everything about the description implies leisure, money, and wealth—the accoutrements of his class. One can have snowy-white cuffs, closely clipped gray hair, and long pink fingernails only if one has not only the money to care for them but also the leisure to keep them that way. Bazarov, on the other hand, had just given his dusty coat and wretched traveling bag to be taken to his room.

Pavel's sensitivity to class lines is immediately apparent: he does not offer his hand to Bazarov but instead deliberately puts both hands in his pocket, and a few minutes later he calls Bazarov "that hairy fellow" (21). Bazarov, too, takes an immediate dislike to the uncle, and after supper he says to Arkady, "Just imagine, such dandyism in the country! Those nails of his, those nails, now—you could send them to an exhibition" (22). And, "I couldn't stop looking at him: what amazing collars he wears—they look as if they were carved out of stone—and his chin is so painstakingly shaved. Isn't it absurd, Arkady Nicholaevich?" (22). The clash is initially about clothes and grooming, but these details point to serious items in Bazarov's agenda: the importance of useful work and the disapproval of idleness and privilege. And beyond these items lies the hostility of Bazarov's class to heredity-based privilege and everything that privilege implies toward one's fellow human beings and the destiny of Russia. Although the conflict between Bazarov and Pavel will be unremitting, Turgenev sketches it first with the seemingly trivial details of clothes and grooming.

An open confrontation between Pavel and Bazarov does not take place immediately, despite the instant dislike of one for the other. Even the following morning open conflict between the two is kept at a distance. They do not talk to each other, but Arkady and Pavel talk to each other about Bazarov. We get essential information about him by way of an enthusiastic disciple conveying that information to an unsympathetic listener. So far we have had no essential information about Bazarov, and what we know about him has come from a few descriptive traits and the few words he has spoken. While Bazarov is off catching frogs, Pavel, at breakfast, asks Arkady, "What is he?" (29). Arkady enthusiastically responds that Bazarov is a nihilist. Pavel defines *nihilist* as someone who respects nothing, but Arkady corrects him by saying that a nihilist is someone who rejects any authority, who does not accept a single principle on faith, no matter how great the aura of respect that surrounds that principle.

The radicals of the 1850s and 1860s did not describe themselves as "nihilists," but Turgenev coined this term to describe them. It is not an inappropriate term, and Arkady's definition of a nihilist as someone who does not accept anything on faith and who looks at everything from a critical point of view would accurately describe the radicals. Such an attitude privileges one's reason and intellect above tradition, faith, and convention. Because it questions everything, such an attitude is also by its very nature a destabilizing element and revolutionary, especially in a society that has rested on unquestioned principles.

Shortly after this discussion about nihilism, Bazarov appears from his frog-hunting expedition, his coat and trousers muddy and marsh grass clinging to his hat. Pavel, as usual, is exquisitely groomed and dressed, with the appropriate morning wear. The conversation between Bazarov and Pavel at breakfast—their first direct conversation—starts off innocently enough with questions from Pavel about German science, but he is quickly put off by Bazarov's tone in answering the questions. As an aristocrat he is accustomed to deferentiality from those of a lower class, as he considers Bazarov to be. But Bazarov answers him curtly and grudgingly and even yawns at one point. He is surely not honored that Pavel has condescended to talk to him. Pavel perceives Bazarov's actions and words as a series of aggressions against his style of life.

Pavel is offended by what he sees as an honoring of German scientists and a contempt for Russian accomplishments. This small conflict about foreign influences points to a persistent conflict in Russian intellectual life in the nineteenth century between those who welcomed foreign influences and those who resisted them and were content to rely on purely Russian efforts. Bazarov and the radicals of this generation were very much in favor of accepting the best Europe had to offer. Russian intellectuals throughout the nineteenth century—including the radicals of the 1850s and 1860s—were greatly influenced by intellectual movements in the West. Russian intellectual history can be characterized as a conflict between imitating the West and developing its own native resources. This is usually characterized as a conflict between "Westerners" and "Slavophiles." Conservative opinion tended to reject following the West and urge a development of Russia's own spiritual resources; liberal and radical thinking tended to urge Russia to follow Western European models.

Pavel's conservatism comes out in his prickly defense of Russia's own national being and his aggression against the superiority of Western models. One of the traits that distinguished the sons from the fathers was the sons' interest in science. Pavel's generation and the intellectuals of the 1840s were by and large interested in philosophy and literature rather than in science. This is why Pavel in this opening argument defers to such German writers as Goethe and Schiller but disdains contemporary Germans who "now are running to some sort of chemists and materialists" (34). Bazarov answers this denigration of science with one of his most famous pronouncements: "A passable chemist is twenty times more useful than any poet" (35). And when Pavel retorts with the question, "You do not recognize art, then?" (35), Bazarov answers ironically, "The Art of Money-Making or No more Hemorrhoids!" (35). The conversation has deteriorated and is brought to an end with Bazarov's rude question, "What is this—an official investigation?" (35).

We may ask why there exists so much hostility between Pavel and Bazarov. Generational differences alone do not account for the differences, since Nikolay is of the same generation as Pavel and there is no particular hostility between him and Bazarov. Indeed, Nikolay reacts with self-doubt and humility before the new ideas pronounced by his son and Bazarov. There is, of course, the matter of temperament: both Pavel and Bazarov are strong men, sure of themselves, and determined to defend their views on life. Both represent extreme views of different ideologies. In giving us Nikolay and Arkady, it may be that Turgenev is suggesting from the beginning that the generations need not be enemies and that there may exist a middle ground.

We may also ask why Pavel should be threatened by Bazarov's interest in science. There is, of course, the matter of habit, of having been brought up with the sentiments of literature and the logic of philosophy. Science is new and largely foreign to Pavel's view of matters. Science is also by its nature a destabilizing force, and Pavel in his conservatism wants society to remain unchanged. Science is based on a respect for material facts and for conclusions proceeding from the material facts; as such it is at variance with such intangibles as tradition, love, faith, and destiny. Pavel has built his life around a belief in these intangibles. His very identity is intertwined with them. The love of his life was a mysterious woman, whom he could not understand and who left an enduring wound on his soul. When Bazarov says that a

passable chemist is 20 times more useful than any poet, he is summa-
rizing in succinct fashion the disparate poles of their worldviews.

One would have to say that Bazarov comes off the better in their
initial encounter. Bazarov is sure who he is and what he represents. He
is more in command of himself than is Pavel. It is Pavel who asks the
questions; who is irritated, annoyed, and angry; and who starts the
argument. Bazarov is aggressive in his gestures and his remarks, but he
is calmer. He yawns, turns away Pavel's questions with jokes. He
enjoys an emotional advantage over Pavel, because Pavel seems threatened by Bazarov's person and his views, and Bazarov is dismissive and
contemptuous of Pavel's person and views. This first confrontation
between Pavel and Bazarov ends with Bazarov's harsh words and the
intercession of Nikolay Kirsanov, a role he will play throughout the
novel. Arkady, too, chastises Bazarov for being unfair to his uncle and
attempts to soften Bazarov's view of his uncle by telling him his uncle's
life story. The introduction of the story here has several functions: it
suspends the growing conflict between the two men and propels us
forward to the anticipated next encounter. It sheds light not only on
Pavel but also on the novel's major ideological struggle.

Pavel's early career in the military—in contrast to that of his
brother—was one of great success. He was in great demand socially,
especially with women, and was making a brilliant career for himself
when he met and fell in love with Princess R., a mysterious and enigmatic woman given to wild swings of emotion: she "danced until she
would collapse, went off into peals of laughter and joked with young
men, whom she received during the afternoon in the semi-darkness of
her drawing room, while her nights she spent in tears and prayer,
unable to find peace anywhere, and often dashing about her room
until the very morning, wringing her hands in melancholy, or, all pale
and chill, sitting bent over the Book of Psalms" (38).

Pavel Kirsanov met Princess R. at a ball; had danced a mazurka
with her, during the course of which she had not said a single sensible
word; and fell passionately in love with her. His conquest of her did
not cool his ardor, and he continued to be attracted to something inac-
cessible in her. His love for her was not satisfying even when it was
requited, but when she fell out of love with him "he almost went out

of his mind" (40). He resigned his commission and spent four years following her abroad. After his brief reconciliation with her in Baden, she avoided him, and he was forced to return to Russia. His purpose in life left him, and he wandered about Russia for some 10 years. He finally learned that she had died in Paris, and he moved to his brother's country estate, where he continued to live a life of disciplined vigil for his lost love.

Princess R. apparently seized Pavel's heart by the mystery of her being. She was not intelligent (Turgenev speaks of her fatuous conversation), she was not beautiful (only her look was captivating), and she was surely not kind or sympathetic. Pavel was a handsome military man who apparently could have had his choice of women, but he sacrificed his career, his dignity, and eventually his purpose in life to a woman who spurned him and who had no discernible positive traits. The situation has all the earmarks of a Romantic passion; it tells us something about what Pavel's generation was captivated by. There is nothing "logical" or "commonsensical" in his attraction to Princess R. What seems to attract him is her "inaccessibility," not in the physical sense but in the emotional sense. Pavel fell in love with the mystery of personality and served up his life on the altar of that mystery.

Bazarov has only contempt for the love affair and looks on the idle life that followed on the affair as trivial and wasteful. Pavel's life has been largely determined by the mystery of love, and Bazarov dismisses such a love—indeed, all loves—as unmysterious and obvious. Love, for him, is a matter of physiological responses and not one of the soul and fate. For Bazarov, love should be in the service of life, understood as useful progress in material things; for Pavel, life is in the service of love, because love is the completion of personality and the focus of life's mystery. Bazarov's view of life includes unknowns, but no mysteries. We notice how artfully Turgenev interweaves the novel's two structural foci—ideology and love—in this opening scene. They will continue to come into relationship and conflict throughout the novel, and Pavel's story, which at first is easy to dismiss as Romantic gesture, will have echoes in Bazarov's life.

Bazarov's dismissal of love as a matter of physiology will have an ironic ring, since he is fated also to have his life changed by a failed love. Bazarov will not fall in love with an enigmatic and destructive woman but with a woman who will dominate him as thoroughly as Pavel had been dominated by Princess R. What he says about Pavel he could say of himself later: "I would say that a fellow who has staked his entire life on the card of woman's love and who, when that card is trumped, goes all to pieces and sinks to such an extent that he's not fit for anything—a fellow like that is no man, no male" (44).

It is perhaps no structural accident that the first conflict comes to an end with Pavel visiting Fenechka to order tea. Fenechka is destined to play a role in the amatory rivalry between Pavel and Bazarov, however unwillingly. Pavel's visit and the facts of Fenechka's life are a preparation for that role. It is no accident, also, that Bazarov makes her acquaintance on the same day. Pavel and Bazarov will collide not only in their ideas but also in their feelings about Fenechka.

Between the rehearsal for the full conflict between Pavel and Bazarov (which occurs on the morning after Bazarov's arrival) and the bitter confrontation between them, two weeks go by. There are structural reasons for this space of time. An explosion between Bazarov and Pavel is inevitable, and the passage of time provides a build-up to the explosion. The time also gives us an opportunity to see Bazarov at work. After the full blowout, when both men lose their temper, another meaningful discussion between them would not be possible, or at least the discussion could not continue with the same intensity. Turgenev has timed the emotional rhythm so that it reaches a crescendo and then dissipates itself by separation. After the first confrontation the emotional intensity is suspended by the background stories of Pavel and Princess R. and Nikolay's meeting of Fenechka and the passage of two weeks. After the second confrontation a more decisive separation is necessary, and Turgenev has Bazarov go away.

The trip into town is a kind of rehearsal for a different kind of conflict—a conflict with Odintsova. The novel proceeds by way of two collisions: an ideological collision with Pavel and then an amatory one with Odintsova. Both collisions tell us something about Bazarov. Pavel and Odintsova are poles against which Bazarov's character is measured. In a sense he is the winner with Pavel and the loser with Odintsova. In the definition of his character and the determination of his fate, Odintsova is more important than Pavel. The confrontation with Pavel is purely ideological, but the confrontation with Odintsova is one of character and identity. Pavel helps us define what Bazarov believes in; Odintsova helps us determine who Bazarov is. It is to these two confrontations that we have to turn in order to understand Bazarov.

Bazarov is not easy to like: he is coarse in manner, aggressive, contemptuous, arrogant; his fingernails are dirty, and he eats with a peasant's gusto. He seems proud of his bad manners. He reduces love to physiological reactions; nature is a laboratory and not a temple; Raphael is not worth a plug nickel or a copper coin; art is the idle pastime of the rich. He has no respect for tradition, sentiment, love, poetry, music, or even logic. He finds it funny that Arkady's father, a man in his middle forties, should play the cello in the country while his estate is going to ruin. And "art" fares no better. He has Arkady give his father Buchner's *Stoff und Kraft* to read instead of Pushkin's *Gypsies*. He says to Arkady, "Aristocracy, liberalism, progress, principles. . . . My, what a batch of foreign and useless words" (66). He tells him also, "The only important thing is that two times two makes four, while everything else is all bosh" (58). He respects only reason, science, and practical work. The rest is rubbish, especially all of the fine sentiments we pay ourselves for our privileges. And when Arkady asks him if nature is bosh too, he answers, "And nature too is bosh—the way you conceive it. Nature is no temple but a workshop, and man is the worker therein" (58).

Pavel respects art, love, family, tradition, and poetry. He represents tradition, the status quo, and, as he expresses it, "principles." Bazarov wants to clear history—Russian history—of its established institutions. It is not just a question of being against the autocracy; Bazarov is against all those institutions that Pavel puts forth as the bedrock of civilization. Bazarov is uncompromising in his opposition to everything Pavel stands for. At one point he challenges Pavel to come up with one institution that deserves preservation. His rhetoric is perhaps never more extreme: "I'll be ready to agree with you," he adds as he stands up, "whenever you confront me with even one factuality in our present way of life, either domestic or social, which would not provoke total and merciless repudiation" (73). Pavel at first says "millions of them" (73) and then suggests the village commune, the traditional collective way of living among the peasants. Bazarov dismisses this with, "Well, as far as the village commune is concerned, you'd better have a talk with your own brother. The way things look, he has by now had a real taste of the village commune, mutual responsibility, temperance and suchlike pretty doodads" (74). Bazarov is referring to the actual (rather than the idealized) situation among the peasant collectives, which were in fact characterized by drunkenness, laziness, and superstition. Pavel does not protest but suggests then "the family" as an institution worth preserving. Bazarov retorts, "It would be better for your own sake not to go into in detail. You've heard, I guess, about patriarchs who have the first go at their daughters-in-law?" (74). Bazarov has in mind the exploitation sexually of the peasants by the gentry—a reference that is uncomfortably close to the situation in the household, where Pavel's brother has taken a peasant as a mistress.

Bazarov is bold and iconoclastic, and the reader is probably with him in his rejection of idleness, aristocratic principle, and the kind of love affair that immobilized Pavel for life. We may also respect his belief in science and practical work. Our reservations about him have to do with his rudeness, the sharpness of his judgment of others, and his overweening self-assuredness. Whatever our criticisms, however, we may still ask how well the members of the aristocracy shape up against him. Pavel has spent a life doing nothing, playing out a script he wrote for himself in early life of fatal remorse and regret for a great love that failed him or he it. The posture is right out of a Romantic novel. Nikolay Kirsanov is less rigid but also less capable than his brother; he attempts to cope with the affairs of the estate, but not very well. He is a bad manager, the estate is going to pot, and he seems bewildered by the conditions that a changing Russia is thrusting on him. He has also, however tender his feelings, exercised a kind of *droit du seigneur* in taking Fenechka as his mistress. Arkady is something of an echo of Bazarov, without ideas of his own. It is clear that his convictions belong to the passing phase of youth—a rebellion unchastened by deep thought and dedication. And in the course of the novel

Arkady comes to give up his "radical" ideas and retreat to the privileges and comforts of his class.

Bazarov, in contrast to these aristocrats, is self-assured, intelligent, far-seeing, and dedicated to progress. He seems to carry the future with him. Pavel, Nikolay, and Arkady, too, are in the final analysis concerned primarily with their privileges. They have done little; Bazarov promises much.

11

Bazarov and His Principles

Whatever admiration and respect we have for Bazarov and his dedication to hard facts, science, and work, it would seem that in his rejection of art, music, love, personality, principles, and even logic he has gone too far. He is against far more than the privileges of the autocracy; he is against almost everything that we, even today, would consider to be the foundation of civilization. An unqualified admiration for Bazarov entails justifying the extreme positions that he occupies, and the positions are not easy to justify. We can ask how an honest and intelligent man can be against principles. Principles would seem to be the cement that holds a civilization together; a man without principles would seem to be someone who has no values and who is committed to selfish gain. Is it possible to be a decent man without espousing certain principles? Indeed, the adjective *unprincipled* describes someone who is dishonorable and indecent.

The radical critic Dmitri Pisarev in his essay "Bazarov" addressed this issue, arguing that one can be honest, hard-working, and even self-sacrificing, even if one rejects, as Bazarov does, all principles. Pisarev says that Bazarov is guided not by principles but only by self-interest and practical reason. Despite this Bazarov does not steal, is hard-working, and acts decently. He does so, says Pisarev, because it is to his interest not to steal and to work hard. He is guided by enlightened self-interest and would no more steal than he would eat rotten meat. To be self-interested does not mean that one is dedicated to hurting others. Self-interest and the interest of others are not in contradiction. The implication of Pisarev's argument is that the new man, such as Bazarov, does not need "principles" in the accepted sense—that is, truths given to him—to lead a decent and honorable life. Reason and enlightened self-interest can guide a man's life better than "principles" in the sense of assumed and unexamined truths.

Pisarev has a point in questioning that we need "principles" in order to act in a civilized manner. The implication of Pavel's position is that in order to be decent a man needs to be "coerced" by some truth outside of his own judgment and reason. For what is a principle? A principle is something above changing circumstance and self-interest, something timeless and presumably for that reason true. Principles are what lift us above the selfish and indulgent side of our character and permit us to live for the common good. Principles may be such things as honesty, love of country, sacrifice for others, working for the common good, love of one's neighbor. We expect an honorable person to adhere to these truths or principles whatever the circumstances and conditions. Indeed, the test of character is the ability to adhere to principles such as these and to resist the shift and tide of conditions.

Principles, however, are also general, inflexible, unmodifiable by circumstances and individual needs. Bazarov does not think that anything is above the corrosion of time, or unmodifiable by circumstances or beyond the analysis of reason and utility. To stand on principles, as does Pavel, is to abdicate the analytic mind, to put some of life beyond questioning and decision and beyond our ability to change matters. An obedience to "principles" may be, according to Bazarov, at times a mindless acquiescence to decisions made by others or formed by habit and custom. Pavel asks us not to question certain things. But Bazarov believes that everything should be questioned, and questioned within the context of the here and now and the specific conditions of the moment. And there is even more. Principles are often covert privileges, especially that of class. Every class, as Marx reminded us, tends to universalize its privileges, to make what benefits itself into something that is unchangeable and beyond question. Pavel is for principles because they serve his privileged life—a life that he would prefer not be questioned or subject to analysis and possible change. One of his principles is to discipline himself in the country by wearing immaculate clothes, even though there is no social reason to do so. But to observe such a principle and discipline one needs money and leisure.

Another of Pavel's principles is devotion to art, and he would seem to have our acquiescence in the sacredness of this principle. Even Turgenev said in one of his letters that he shared all of Bazarov's views except those on art. How can one be against art? It is presumably the flower of man's perception and understanding of the world; it unites the seen and the unseen and gives us all insight into the past and into the lives of others. It is presumably what unites us as a people, yet it is also something freighted with class privilege. We know that art has been commissioned to praise and honor those who have had the wherewithal to command its creation and pay for it. We know, too, that art requires many conditions that make it necessarily the activity of those who have the time and leisure to practice it. Such conditions obviously are available to the dominant class, and the reverence for art may be a veil for the distinction of one class from another.

True though this may be, this does not exclude the possibility that members of the gentry are sincere in their admiration of art. Shortly after the second and irremediable conflict between Bazarov and Pavel is a scene that points up this fact. Nikolay, who has listened carefully to the argument between Pavel and Bazarov, is sincerely shaken in his belief in art and nature. Shortly after the argument he takes a walk in his garden and in his favorite arbor reflects on the possibility that his generation is wrong: "Doesn't their superiority consist of their having fewer traces of seigniory than we? He let his head sink and ran his hand over his face. But—to reject poetry, he again reflected. To have no feeling for art, for nature" (76). He looks about him, and the scene is one of natural beauty at dusk. It is clear that Nikolay's heart responds to the beauty about him: "My God, how fine all this is! Nikolay reflected, and some favorite lines came to his lips, but at this point he recalled Arkady, and *Stoff und Kraft*—and fell silent" (77).

Nikolay's reverie is interrupted by the arrival of Fenechka, a reminder that his love of art and nature is paralleled and perhaps reinforced by the sincere love he feels for her. A short time later we have a parallel scene with Pavel in the same garden: "Pavel walked on until he came to the end of the garden and he, too, fell into deep thought; he, too, raised his eyes to heaven. However, nothing was reflected in his splendid dark eyes except the light of the stars. No born romantic, he, and his gallantly dry soul, misanthropic after the French manner, was incapable of indulging in reveries" (80). Nikolay feels sincerely the beauty of nature and of art; nothing is reflected in Pavel's eyes but the light of the stars—nothing penetrates those eyes to his soul. Turgenev may have inserted this scene to undercut any facile judgment we might want to make about the generations.

As part of his worldview Bazarov has a democratic thrust, the desire to reconstruct the world for the benefit of the many and not of the few. He also has as part of his worldview a strong utilitarian thrust, as did his real-life prototypes. One of his real-life radical prototypes, Chernyshevsky, as we have seen, questioned the necessity of art at all. In his notorious 1855 essay "The Aesthetic Relations of Art to Reality" he asked the point of painting a woman when a real woman exists or painting an apple when a real apple exists. Chernyshevsky makes a powerful case against "iconicizing" art and removing it from the real concerns of history and human need. At bottom he is arguing for a human art—one that serves human and historical needs—and against those who would place it above and beyond human interests and concerns. There seems little doubt that Turgenev had Chernyshevsky's work in mind in expressing Bazarov's views on art, as he also seems to have had in mind the views of Pisarev, who called for the destruction of esthetics on the same grounds and questioned money being spent on art when there were more pressing needs, such as hunger, housing, and education.[27]

We are likely to have been so schooled in the sacredness of "culture" that such opinions are automatically dismissed as nonsense. Yet it is difficult to respond with persuasive arguments to Chernyshevsky's reasoning and its encapsulation in the rhetoric of Bazarov. It may be also that Turgenev shows a kind of class solidarity with Pavel in distancing himself from Bazarov on the question of art's importance. Later in the nineteenth century Leo Tolstoy was to add his powerful voice to those who questioned the importance of art. In *What Is Art?* (1898) Tolstoy was to argue, somewhat in the vein of Chernyshevsky (and Bazarov), that Western art was elitist, trivial, and even morally corrupting. The point here is that Bazarov's "outrageous" statements about art are not a willful eccentricity that Turgenev gives to his hero but a position that comes from a strong tradition in Russian critical thought questioning art along the same lines.

Nor is Bazarov's argument in his own terms without logic and defense. Bazarov employs some of the same outrageous rhetoric in speaking of art as did Chernyshevsky and Pisarev. He privileges science over art (Buchner over Pushkin), ridicules a middle-aged nobleman—Nikolay Kirsanov—passing his time playing a cello, and says Raphael is not worth a plug nickel. If one responds that utility is a crude way by which to judge art, then Bazarov would point to the fact that art, no matter how judged, is necessarily a product of privileged people and conditions. Art is always guided by someone's usefulness. It is never free of specific conditions and historical needs. Art carries the past with it and is a codification of past feelings and attitudes. It is a product of past circumstances and historical conditions, and as such it is captive of the past and of class relations. It is the product of those who have had the time and money to produce it, and surely the product of those who shared historically limiting values. Art is a kind of authority, commanding us to think in and feel a particular way, or at least this is the way that the radical critics, and Bazarov, reasoned.

"Art" as something above human criticism is what Bazarov rejects, but there is nothing in his remarks, despite the abusive rhetoric, that suggests he is against another kind of art: a revolutionary art, born of new circumstances, new thought, and new feelings. It would have to be an art close to the people and serve the needs of all the people and not just of an elitist group. Such an art would have to be in revolt against institutionalizing itself and capturing the future with the authority of the past. Nor is there anything in his views that would reject "principles" in the sense of certain values such as honesty, sacrifice, and duty to others. Indeed, Bazarov seems to have a direct honesty about him; he displays no equivocation or insincerity. He is in fact probably the most direct and honest person in the novel. By his work he clearly intends to sacrifice much of his time and effort for the good of humanity. It is not so much that he is against such principles as honesty, sacrifice, and the common good as he is against particular conceptions thereof. He is against unquestioned and untried principles; he would surely be in favor of principles that endure the pragmatic tests of time and reason.

Fathers and Sons is very much a novel of conflicting class positions, and to ignore these positions is to misread the novel. As a *raznochinets* Bazarov has a "fluid" class position—he is outside the privileges of name and wealth. To reject the gentry's standards is to confirm his outsiderness. He cannot afford to keep his fingernails as beautiful as Pavel's. The rudeness Bazarov shows toward Pavel's rules of politeness is less ignorance on Bazarov's part and more a mode of rejection of what such "manners" imply. Pavel speaks of personality and the discipline necessary to keep up one's sense of self even in the country. But such manners are ritualized gestures to separate oneself from those who are not part of the social group that practices such manners.

Pavel is very much aware of the class differences. Indeed, when he is first told that Bazarov is going to stay with them, he refers to him as the "hairy-one," the ill-kempt one, stressing immediately the differences of grooming. Nor is he satisfied until he can identify Bazarov's class. Bazarov, he repeats to himself; he had known a provincial doctor in the army whose name was Bazarov. He is not satisfied until has identified Bazarov's father and their respective class. The point of all this is that the enmity between Pavel and Bazarov may be one partly of temperament, but it also is a matter of class struggle. Pavel is defending his class privileges, and Bazarov is rejecting them.

We must keep in mind that *Fathers and Sons* is about a period in Russian history when the traditional patriarchal class arrangements (gentry and peasants) are breaking down in part. And it is the gentry that is feeling under siege. Arkady can afford to be less sharp, more understanding, and more tolerant of his uncle's behavior because he is part of Pavel's world of privilege. Indeed, Arkady tries to be on both sides, but in the end he closes ranks with the aristocracy. At the beginning of the novel he is a student who has not yet assumed fully his class status. But during the progress of the novel he comes to accept the values that assure his class privileges. Nikolay, too, despite the mildness of his temperament acts and thinks in a way that defends his class. It is possible, too, that class status plays a role in Odintsova's rejection of Bazarov.

Bazarov does not have much space between peasants and aristocrats to pursue his own advantage. He belongs to an emerging class that has been shut out of the privileges and powers of the society. Bazarov has been trained as a doctor, but his brilliance far outreaches the kind of life that his doctor father leads. He cannot be part of the aristocracy and as a consequence not part of those who rule Russia, and by his talent and ambition he cannot be just a provincial doctor. Bazarov cannot live like Pavel, and he cannot live like Nikolay and Arkady, but his father's property is too modest.

Bazarov feels considerable frustration, and some of it comes from the confines of the social system in which he must live and work. The space between peasant and master is small, and it is no surprise that he wants change and Pavel does not—indeed, none of the aristocrats wants change. To be sure, Arkady has the typical youthful stage of rebellion against the fathers, which manifests itself in his admiration for Bazarov, but once away from school and back in his native habitat he settles quickly into the patrician life-style. The frustrations of Bazarov's class background are to be seen also in his relationship with Odintsova. Odintsova is nobility, even if the comforts and privileges of her noble status were seriously jeopardized by her profligate father. She is also representative of how the edges of privilege are being nibbled away by the times. She is able to maintain these privileges only by certain sacrifices, and specifically by submerging her feelings and marrying someone who is repulsive to her. Because she almost lost the prerequisites of her class by way of changed circumstances, she is sensitive to the winds of change. Bazarov fascinates her, and she goes to the edges of her fantasy until her class consciousness draws her back.

In that narrow path Bazarov has open to him, he is equally excluded by the masters and the peasants. He uses his closeness to the peasants as something of a club to beat Pavel with. Indeed, he does talk to them, and the young peasant boys are more comfortable with him than they are with the masters, as is Fenechka. The peasants see him as part of the masters, however, and he has considerable contempt for them and their superstitions. He has no intention of iconicizing the peasants, "the people," as the aristocracy had traditionally done. There is nothing of the "repentant nobleman" about him, and he reflects much of Pisarev's view of the peasant as the stomach of the nation. Bazarov embodies much of the frustration of the "in-between class," which has been educated and have nowhere to apply their intellectual strength unless the society changes. Is it any surprise that they want society to change radically?

In the heat of his argument with Pavel, Bazarov's position and his remarks are more extreme and less defensible than they would be otherwise. When Pavel asks him what the constructive side of his program is, he remarks contemptuously that destruction and not construction is what he is concerned with. But a remark of this kind is calculated to shock and aggravate Pavel. Bazarov is no destroyer for destruction's sake, no more so than his real-life prototypes. He is for certain things, and they are important; although he does not put forth a program, he has a position, a view of a better way of organizing life than it has been up to now. But he does not have a program, a set of beliefs that one "canonizes" and adheres to unthinkingly. All programs are condemned to be formulated and as such to be finished, and the danger is that one can become uncritically attached to "programs." A program, too, can be an "authority" and as such can be placed above the concrete circumstances in which one finds oneself.

Bazarov wants a process by which one refuses to accept anything uncritically. This is why at one point he dismisses even "logic," an extraordinary statement for one who seems attached to rational inquiry. But Bazarov understands that logic, too, can be iconicized, lifted above the circumstances where a practical reason can subject it to critical inquiry. It is not that he is for or against "logic"; it all depends on whether one worships logic as an authority or whether one uses logic to some end. He is no more against logic than he is against honesty, love, decency, fairness. But he is against all universals. He understands, however, that all such values vary with the times and with those in power who establish what they are. His point is simply that these values, whatever they are, should not be blindly and unthinkingly accepted but should pass a critical or rational test.

Bazarov's views clearly indicate a privileging of "reason" as a pragmatic instrument, operating for the benefit of the people, presumably all the people and not only a few. There is, too, the modest assumption that one cannot elevate the present values into universals. One cannot predict what the circumstances will be and what "values" will be necessary in different circumstances. This is the part of his answer to Pavel about what values he would put in place of the present ones. He cannot enunciate universal principles because they do not exist except as covert manipulations of power and authority. Given all these caveats, it is still fair to ask what Bazarov's vision is of the better life in the present circumstances in which he lives.

This position on universals and the use of reason for practical purposes represent a general change in philosophy. In his first conversation with Arkady about Bazarov, Pavel had referred to Hegel as a factor in Russian intellectual life. Arkady had just told Pavel that Bazarov was a nihilist, and Pavel had said, "Yes. Before we had the Hegelists, but now we have the nihilists" (30). Hegel's influence on Russian thought from the early 1830s to the mid-1850s was immense, especially in the work of Herzen and Belinsky. The influence was on the "fathers," and it is Hegel's legacy that the radicals were determined to overthrow. Chernyshevsky devotes a substantial part of "The Aesthetic Relations of Art to Reality" to demolishing Hegelian thought.

What the Russians took from Hegel (and other German idealistic thinkers) is the belief in a universal reason that unfolded itself in the progress of history. Russian intellectuals were very attracted to this belief because it conferred on history a rational necessity and the consequent unreality of what appeared to be random chance in empirical reality. One could speak of a "logic" of history, and it is precisely this kind of logic Bazarov has in mind when he slights it. It is not that Bazarov or his radical prototypes dismissed reason; rather, they preferred another kind of reason: a practical reason. What they had in mind was a reason acting on historical circumstances, and they rejected their fathers' belief in a reason that operated independently of those circumstances or a reason that commanded a specific reality. They considered the Hegelian program mysterious and unreal.

In short, then, when Bazarov rejects logic he is not being destructive, at least not willfully destructive. He has in mind the logic of his fathers, and he favors in a constructive fashion a practical reason directed at practical and attainable ends. Bazarov does have constructive ends if not a constructive program. He does not have a program in Pavel's sense, because such a program would be built on unquestioned "principles" or "beliefs" and as such would be in keeping with Pavel's position. Bazarov is, after all, in favor of science, which is a set of procedures for understanding nature and, on its pragmatic side, a set of investigations calculated and intended to make human life better. He is for work as against idleness, against privilege, and for democratic opportunities. He is against unquestioned beliefs or principles and for a questioning of all established truths. Most of all, he is for a pragmatic view of life and an alleviation of hunger, waste, and human misery. He is, we can assume, against class privilege and for democracy. There is a material substratum to much of what Bazarov says, so that when Pavel asks in astonishment, "How so?" (67), to Bazarov's dismissal of logic, Bazarov answers that you do not need logic to pop a hunk of bread into your mouth when you are hungry. He speaks in similar material and biological terms when he refers to love.

How do we square Bazarov's belief in reason with this physiological or material approach? Again for rhetorical purposes, Bazarov puts forth his materialism in an aggressive and vulgar way, but, like Chernyshevsky, he is an unquestioned materialist in that he rejects any realm of being above material nature. Bazarov and the radical critics do not believe in "spiritual values" in the sense of values that are validated by a realm of reality above matter. Bazarov is interested in human dignity and all the values we associate therewith, as based on material values. Bazarov and the radical critics were "monists" in the sense that they rejected all dualisms, the most familiar of which is the belief in the existence of a material and spiritual world. Furthermore, they believed such dualisms to be not only untrue but also a source of misery and deprivation in men's lives. They were persuaded that a belief in the thoroughgoing nature of our material beings and the application of a practical reason to this material nature would result not only in the dispelling of superstitions about man's nature but also in the betterment of man's life, presumably because man will act in conformity with his real nature and needs.

12

Sitnikov and Kukshina

Bazarov's position is to some extent strengthened in the novel by contrasting him to others who hold some of the same views. Arkady begins the novel by agreeing with and echoing Bazarov, and the reader quickly sees that Bazarov brings an intelligence and seriousness to his ideas that Arkady does not possess. Arkady has been caught up in the fashion of the radical ideas that Bazarov represents, and part of his function in the novel—at least in the early parts—is to show, by contrast, how serious, complex, and profound are Bazarov's thoughts and beliefs. This is even more true of two other characters—Sitnikov and Kukshina—whose superficiality and fashion-mongering set off the seriousness and depth of Bazarov's radicalism. It is Turgenev's way of recognizing that every movement attracts imitators and degraders.

Sitnikov is a follower of Bazarov, and in this sense he is in a parallel position with Arkady. He is present to show that Bazarov's ideas can be misused. Some of that has already been shown by Arkady, who uses Bazarov's positions too readily and too automatically. On several occasions Bazarov frowns when Arkady speaks for him. Still, despite the similarities, Arkady is not Sitnikov. Sitnikov and Kukshina are static characters. Unlike Arkady, they undergo no change in their character or beliefs. They play no independent role in the novel, and Sitnikov especially is an example of "mindless" espousal and use of Bazarov's ideas. When we first meet him he tells Arkady that he is a disciple of Bazarov's and owes his regeneration to Bazarov. He recalls that when he heard Bazarov declare that one need not respect authorities, he experienced rapture. Bazarov does not want to inspire emotional rapture but rather to effect practical changes in people's lives. Sitnikov in his admiration of Bazarov is a throwback to the kind of emotionalism that was often substituted for action by the previous generation. Bazarov's position is one of great complexity, but Turgenev makes it clear by way of first Arkady and now Sitnikov that the position can degenerate in the use of certain slogans.

Kukshina is a female Sitnikov. She is presented to us in an unattractive manner: she is disheveled and dressed in a silk dress that is not quite tidy. Her drawing room is filled with thick magazines that are, for the most part, not cut—that is, not read. She smokes, gossips, and drops names at a rapid pace. She refers to Emerson, George Sand, Bunsen, Fenimore Cooper, Macaulay, Proudhon, and Michelet and is clearly at pains to impress Bazarov. At the ball we are told rather gratuitously that her gloves are dirty. Turgenev seems to want to make some analogy between the untidiness of her person and surroundings and the untidiness of her mind. Still, her defense of women has a note of sincerity and passion, even though her words provoke no assent from those present. At the time Turgenev was writing *Fathers and Sons* a nascent women's movement existed in Russia. Women were appearing in society alone, attending the universities, and demanding some of the traditional privileges of men. To be sure, Kukshina is a caricatured representation of such an emancipated woman, and the fact that Turgenev chose to present us with a representative of a liberated woman in that guise may tell us something of his attitude toward the nascent movement.

Bazarov, as an example of the radical generation, treats Kukshina with indifferent contempt; indeed, his remarks about women throughout the novel are denigrating and even degrading, with the exception of his relationship with Odintsova, although his initial remarks about her are also degrading and contemptuous. Here Turgenev departs from historical reality, since Bazarov's prototypes looked on women with great respect and championed their cause. In *What Is to Be Done?* Chernyshevsky portrays liberated women and champions both occupational and sexual equality for women. Since Turgenev knew the works of Chernyshevsky well, one must conclude that he gave Bazarov such negative views of women in order to denigrate Bazarov. Turgenev himself had enlightened attitudes toward women, even though these attitudes had an idealized tone to them. It is perhaps no accident that in Anna Odintsova he gives us a woman of character, intelligence, and self-worth.

Despite the fact that Turgenev presents Kukshina in an unattractive light, however, we feel a certain pity for her. She seems alone in the luncheon scene in which we meet her. None of the men present—including the man of the future, Bazarov—treats her various opinions seriously. Arkady is offended by the crudeness of the luncheon, and in the end he is the first to ask to leave. Bazarov, on the other hand, busies himself with eating and drinking and behaving largely with indifference to Kukshina's opinions and Sitnikov's antics.

In giving us these two caricatured liberals, Turgenev seems to be doing several things: he qualifies any impulse the reader may have to regard Bazarov's radicalism in an uncritical way. He seems to be saying that there are radicals like Bazarov and there are radicals like Sitnikov and Kukshina. There are bright and talented radicals; there are mediocre and fair-weather radicals like Arkady; and there are stupid radicals like Kukshina and Sitnikov. It is a way of distancing us from generalizations about political positions in somewhat the same way he has distanced us from generalizations about the aristocracy. We have a rigid and unfeeling aristocrat in Pavel Kirsanov, and we have a feeling and sensitive aristocrat in Nikolay Kirsanov. It is not that Turgenev wishes us to regard impassively differences of political positions. He did, after all, align himself in his public statements with Bazarov and not with the aristocrats, but he wants us to be attentive to the fact that behind the political position is a person, and that the position will be as wise or stupid as is the person. Part of the structure of the novel involves the placing of the different characters along the axis of radical and conservative. Turgenev has so structured the novel that there is no easy and simple correlation of ideological position and truth. If the radical politics of Bazarov are to be admired, then Kukshina and Sitnikov are there to show that those positions can be caricatured and distorted.

13

Odintsova

The change that the various characters undergo during the course of the novel is an important structural consideration. Arkady, for example, moves in a predictable fashion—from student experimentation and safe and verbal radicalism to the social conservatism of his class. Pavel does not move at all; he is at the end what he was at the beginning—an inflexible defender of his class privilege. Odintsova shows some emotional vacillation during the course of her relationship with Bazarov, but in the end she repeats what she has done at the beginning—she marries someone who will not impinge on her emotional life but will bolster her class position. Sitnikov and Kukshina are brought into the novel as caricatured representatives of the liberal and radical politics and then disappear, playing no essential role. Nikolay and his son Arkady show some initial reflection on their status and social position but retreat to the life they have always known. It is only Bazarov who undergoes a profound transformation: he changes from a fearless defender of a new social system to a bitter cynic. At the end he seems to be contemptuous of social change, hates his fellow man, and seems to welcome death. The change would seem to throw into question the sincerity and worth of his ideological position at the beginning and to provoke the reader to find a cause for the change.

The picture of Bazarov is double: a Bazarov of aggressive confidence and a Bazarov of despair and disillusion; of faith in himself and of doubt and despair; one who is life-giving and one who seeks death. The Bazarov of the first half of the novel is aggressive and confident, and the Bazarov of the last third of the novel—who follows his father aimlessly in the rounds of his duty and who foolishly and needlessly permits himself to be infected by a dirty lancet—is spiritually bankrupt. Something happens to Bazarov between the beginning and the end, something serious enough to change radically his view of the world and of himself. The fulcrum between these two Bazarovs is his meeting and failed love for Anna Odintsova.

The image of Bazarov as the representative of revolutionary dynamism or as the best of humanity's struggle against decadence, sloth, and recalcitrant nature can be maintained only if one ignores that substantial part of the novel in which he falls in love with Odintsova, is rejected by her, and is transformed in character and vision. The change is not small; it goes to the very core of his being. Before his meeting and failed love for her, he is coarse, gruff, confident, virile, and in magnificent command of himself. After he meets and is rejected by her, he becomes unsure of himself and cynical about the very values he seemed to champion in the first part of the novel. He becomes debilitated in spirit, uncertain in motive, weary and cynical; in the end he commits a passive suicide. This momentous change from moral and psychological virility and health to spiritual bankruptcy has not been honestly confronted by most critics. The critic P. G. Pustovojt has asked the question, "Where do such pessimism, skepticism, such joylessness and lack of perspective in the hero's views come from?" (Pustovojt, 174). We see a different Bazarov after his failed love affair with Odintsova. That failed love is at least the proximate cause of his depression, of a growing cynicism, of a lack of purpose.

Much of the novel seems to be constructed on a series of oppositions—Bazarov and Pavel, conservative and radical, fathers and sons, young and old, gentry and peasant, intelligent radicalism (Bazarov) and stupid and fashionable radicalism (Kukshina and Sitnikov)—and, indeed, most of the characters can be disposed along some line of opposition. Odintsova does not fit easily into any of these oppositions. She is of the gentry, but for a time she lost the wealth necessary for gentry status. She is conservative but somewhat radical in her fantasies, and she is attracted to Bazarov in part because of his radical views. She has none of the rigid and passionate defense of privilege that characterizes Pavel, but she also has none of the passionate ideological nature of Bazarov, not to mention his rough social mannerisms. Although Bazarov charges the gentry with sentimentality and romantic inclinations, Odintsova clearly does not fit this definition. She is very much a realist and rationalist, and part of the difficulty Bazarov has in his relationship with her comes from the fact that she does not fit his presuppositions about women or the gentry.

Odintsova is by far the most substantial of the novel's female figures and may be the only worthy counterpart to Bazarov in terms of intelligence, imagination, and character. We meet her and Kukshina about the same time, and no insistence on the part of Turgenev is needed to tell us which of the two women has character, identity, and depth. The women in the novel are otherwise not a superior lot, and Turgenev, with his excellent sense of the historical moment, may have touched the reality of their situation. Fenechka is the submissive, somewhat frightened mistress and then wife of the gentle Nikolay. As the daughter of a house serf, she represents in her emotions all the fear and timidity the peasant class feels toward its masters, and if she "advances" in her status it is because the master grants such an advance. Princess R., Pavel's fateful love, was clearly a romantic stereotype, and to the extent that she represented a social type her life was dedicated to controlling with her enigmatic behavior those who loved her. She represents how Pavel's generation granted power to women: in the confines of love and salon society.

Kukshina occupies the pathetic position of a possibly talented woman who has, because of society, been excluded from the intellectual and activist role and who is permitted inclusion in it only at the price of service to men. Her intellectual views are not taken seriously by anyone, including Turgenev. The advanced thinking of Bazarov has no place for an "advanced" woman, or indeed even tolerance for an intellectual woman. In *What Is to Be Done?* Chernyshevsky wrote of women who were the equal of men in vision and intelligence and in work for the construction of a better society. But Turgenev's picture of Kukshina was probably more accurate than Chernyshevsky's Vera, and Bazarov's contemptuous and cruel dismissal of her was also probably an accurate picture of how men in the advanced movements treated women.

Turgenev treated women in life with inordinate respect, and they were for him creatures of great mystery and power. He never lost his awe of the opposite sex, despite the lifetime he spent being hopelessly in love with Pauline Viardot, an opera singer he met in November 1843. Admired and feted by kings and queens, Pauline was not pretty—in fact, she was almost ugly and had a sullen demeanor. She was accompanied by Chopin and Liszt; Alfred de Musset asked for her hand in marriage; and George Sand used her as a model for her novel *Consuelo*. Turgenev's devotion to Pauline was not reciprocated, however, though his ardor apparently had its effect: they may have had an affair in 1844 when she returned to Russia for more appearances. He resigned his job in the Russian civil service, moved to Europe, and became her devotee until he died in 1883.

His female characters, too, are by and large strong. Rudin fails at the moment of crisis, and Natalya shows the strength to give herself to the moment and to her love. Liza in *A Nest of Gentlefolk* has a quiet center that Lavretsky is never able to find. And Elena in *On the Eve* shows fierce dedication to her love and to a political cause at the expense of comfort, family, and country. Turgenev tended to dramatize women trapped in traditional roles, attempting to reach out to something beyond their assigned subservient status. He does this without violating realism and the actual conditions of the time; because of this, the efforts of his female characters are often shown to be eccentric, incomplete, and extreme.

Very few avenues were open to women in Turgenev's society, and they were able to break out of their assigned roles only by violating expectations. He shows, also, conventional women, sometimes likable and charming persons, who are content with their place in society. As an author he is always the objective observer, though trapped himself in attitudes that are conventional and aristocratic. Although his conventional views are apparent, they are not permitted to distort his description of that circumstances about him. Odintsova and her sister Katya are strong women, Odintsova more so than Katya. Katya is shown to be stronger than Arkady, but it is also clear that she will be permitted to use that strength only in the traditional roles of wife and mother. Odintsova, too, is shown to be constrained by the social structure of the time. She can make her way in this society only by marriages that are rational and even calculating. Still, she is the most interesting woman in the novel.

There is no doubt that Odintsova holds her feelings in check in everything but fantasy, that she is willing to risk little, that she is frightened by excessive emotion, and that she withdraws easily into the carapace of habit and routine. Still, she has accomplished a great deal. She had once lost what were the prerequisites of her class, and she had to pay dearly to regain them—she had to marry someone she did not love and endure provincial gossip. Furthermore, she had been placed in such straits by the man she had trusted and loved—her father. Left alone with a younger sister on her hands and few resources, she found the strength, intelligence, and practical wisdom to preserve her dignity and class position. She did not marry the older nobleman from cynicism or depravity but from necessity. She had learned that those who love you can hurt you, and that her place and security were not immune to chance and accident. She is intelligent and self-possessed enough to not let this happen again. The epithet *cold* that never leaves the lips of critics characterizing her and that is always a term of rebuke overlooks that "coldness" is the reserve of those who have been hurt and have learned to risk little.

There is nothing to indicate that Odintsova is the flirt she has been charged with being, but having been used by men—both her father and her first husband—she is probably not beyond using them. That apart, she is kind, patient, honest, and incorrigibly courteous. Furthermore, she is genuinely interested in and attracted to Bazarov, whose intense nature could not fail to touch that part of herself which she had held in restraint. It is possible, too, that his indeterminate class position touches that edge of risk that she admired in her father and which for a time called out the best in her. She has indeed many of the traits that the radicals of the 1850s and Bazarov, as the presumed representative of them, admired: independence of mind, discipline, self-possession. To these we can add the best of her class in courtesy, dignity, and consideration of others.

During her last conversation with Bazarov, Odintsova explains the failure of their love by the enigmatic statement that they were too much alike. And they are. They are alike in a rational view of reality and most of all in the attempt to control the circumstances of their lives. If they share the trait of dispassionate assessment of reality and an unsentimental will to act on reality for their own interest, then it is clear that Odintsova is more successful at it than is Bazarov. She conducts herself throughout the relationship with grace, good taste, and honor. The same cannot be said of Bazarov. This is true from their first meeting.

After the bitter argument with Pavel, Bazarov leaves with Arkady for a provincial town to pay respects to the governor. There they meet Sitnikov and Kukshina, and after that meeting they go to a provincial ball, where they meet Odintsova. The first description of Odintsova is that of a beautiful woman: she has gleaming hair, sloping shoulders, radiant eyes, and a svelte waist. But she also has a "dignity of bearing," "her radiant eyes looked calmly and intelligently," and "some sort of kindly and gentle power emanated from her face" (98). We are told immediately that there is something more to her than a beautiful body. In fact, her beauty is not without blemish: her nose is a trifle bulbous and her complexion is not altogether clear. What is most striking about her is the quiet power that emanates from her being. Even Bazarov admits on first seeing her that she does not resemble the rest of the females at the ball.

Odintsova is, too, strikingly at ease with everyone she talks to, whatever their social standing. She listens to Arkady with polite sympathy, dances without comment with the fool Sitnikov, and chats "just as unconstrainedly with her dancing partner as with the grandee" (99). She does not need the easy and self-indulgent irony that characterizes Bazarov's dismissal of Sitnikov and Kukshina: "She herself did not say much, yet her words evinced a knowledge of life; from certain comments of hers Arkady concluded that this young woman had already come to experience a great deal emotionally and to think over many things" (100).

Odintsova had noticed Bazarov early in the evening and asks Arkady about him. She listens without comment to Arkady's excited and passionate exposition of Bazarov's views but adds, when she invites Arkady to visit her, "You may as well bring your friend with you. I'll find it extremely curious to see a man who has the temerity not to believe in anything" (101). Bazarov's effect on her is one of quiet curiosity; her effect on him is to provoke him to aggressive disparagement of her. Bazarov talks about her to Arkady in ribald and salacious tones. He makes a point of noticing her shoulders: "She's got a pair of shoulders on her the like of which I haven't laid my eyes on in a long time" (102). He insinuates that her "calm" is a case of still waters running deep: "She's cold, you say. That's precisely what the piquancy consists of. After all, you're fond of frozen sweets" (102). And he disparages not only Odintsova but all women. In response to Arkady's statement that there is freedom of thought among women, he says, "Because, brother, according to what I have observed, among women it is only the freaks who think freely" (102).

At the hotel the next day it is no better for Bazarov: he is ill at ease in Odintsova's presence, he blushes, and he continues to belittle her by sexual allusion when he is not in her presence. He refers to her as "the duchess" (107) and disparages her class and life-style. It is only her persistent courtesy, politeness, and graciousness that work to soften what one must take as insecurity on his part. Only when he has been reassured by her flattery and respect for him is he capable of returning something resembling mature behavior. It is clear—and it is a surprise to Arkady—that Odintsova holds in some way an emotional advantage over Bazarov, and that he reveals considerable insecurity in her presence. His disparagement of her is his way of dealing with his own weakness. Out of her presence, he reverts to sexual belittling by referring several times to her "opulent body" (108). Bazarov's fascination with her is seen in the alacrity with which he agrees to go with Arkady for a visit to her country house.

During Arkady and Bazarov's brief visit with Odintsova at the hotel, Turgenev interrupts the narrative in his characteristic fashion to give us a brief summary of Odintsova's life. Her father was a gambler who lost most of the family's money and on his death left a minuscule estate to his two daughters, 20-year-old Anna and 12-year-old Katya. Their mother having died earlier, Anna found herself with little money, the care of her younger sister, and the management of the estate. It is revealing that she did not lose her head but sent for an aunt (to provide the respectable conditions and security for two young girls living alone). Shortly thereafter she married a rich and unattractive man. He died six years later, leaving Anna with considerable property. There was considerable gossip about her marriage and about her character, but Anna remained indifferent to most of it.

The first thing that strikes visitors to Odintsova's estate is the reigning order. Her discussions with Bazarov touch on some of the same topics that Bazarov and Pavel's earlier discussions had, but the temper and outcome of the discussions are different. Although there is intensity to both encounters, the former quickly becomes acrimonious and unpleasant, whereas the latter is serious and calm. Nor is this to be explained by a lack of differences. As with Pavel, Bazarov expresses his indifference to "art," and Odintsova voices her appreciation of art. It is to her that he expresses an extreme view about the value of personality. He says, "All people resemble one another in both body and soul; in each one of us the brain, the spleen, the heart, the lungs are arranged in the same way, and the moral qualities, so-called, are precisely the same in all. . . . People are as uniform as trees in a forest: no botanist would go to the trouble of studying each individual birch" (113). Anna shakes her head at an opinion she does not agree with but continues the discussion calmly by saying, "Therefore, according to you, there is no difference between a foolish man and an intelligent one, between a good man and one who is evil" (114). Bazarov, following his radical predecessors, answers by saying that the difference is one of health and sickness: "Reform society, and there won't be any maladies" (114).

The calm with which Odintsova carries on this discussion is a sign of self-possession and security, surely not of indifference. She is intelligent, well-read, and interested in the topics that are raised before her. Bazarov, on the other hand, following this reasoning, is probably not as secure in his beliefs and reasoning, since, like Pavel, he is quick and extreme in defending them. Despite his increasing respect for Anna, Bazarov cannot refrain from making disparaging remarks about her. He acknowledges that she is a "female with brains" (119) but quickly qualifies this by calling her a shop-worn article. Anna, in the meantime, becomes increasingly attracted to Bazarov, enjoying his obvious intelligence, his lack of flirtatiousness, and even the harshness of his judgments. Although Arkady is attracted to her in a slavish and sophomoric way, Odintsova takes no advantage of his attraction and politely and courteously ignores it.

Most characteristic about Odintsova is her lack of perturbation. She seems to lead and desire an unruffled life. Turgenev says of her, "Her mind was searching and, at the same time, apathetic: her doubts were never lulled to forgetfulness and never attained the stature of alarm" (120). And, "Life held ease for her, even though there were times when she felt ennui, and she kept on passing day after day at a leisurely pace and experiencing perturbation only at rare intervals" (120). This even-temperedness and seeming lack of passion is what leads Bazarov to call her cold. Turgenev makes clear, however, that it is less a lack of passion and more a disciplined restraint from giving in to passion. She has a vivid imagination; at times her soul would be filled with instantaneous daring and "would seethe with noble yearning" (120), but these impulses are always overcome by a desire for comfort and ease. It is clear that Bazarov touches some deep reserve of her imagination and longing, and for a time she permits herself the pleasure of possibly sharing a life with him.

What is it in Bazarov that attracts her? Being a person of substance herself, she is clearly attracted to the serious qualities of Bazarov's character and his intelligence. He is different from the men she has known. She had been married for six years to Odintsov, a flabby and fatuous man, and doubtlessly had been courted by others in the meantime. And Bazarov, by his difference in many respects, brings a note of danger and risk into her mind. And that danger may remind her of her father, a gambler and risk-taker. We are told that she loved her father dearly, and something of his recklessness and risk-taking may have remained with her, although deeply buried and only now touched by the possibility of a love for Bazarov. Bazarov is a radical student, comes from a lower class, and has an uncertain future. In the end she does not act on this, retreating into the protective shell she had so carefully constructed for herself.

The problem for Bazarov in his growing attraction to Odintsova is perhaps even more difficult. He is by conviction an enemy of all romantic love and a believer that one's relationship with women is governed by physiological reflexes. The strain on him in meeting an intelligent, disciplined, and self-possessed woman is great. He becomes edgy, restless, and angry in his looks—all emotions that indicate a struggle against other emotions. Turgenev characterizes the struggle in this way: "The real reason for all these 'new' attitudes was a feeling inspired in Bazarov by Odintsova, a feeling which tormented and devilishly infuriated him and which he would have denied on the spot with contemptuous laughter and cynical invective had anyone hinted to him even in a roundabout fashion at the possibility of that which was going on within him" (125).

The feelings between these two come to a climax when Bazarov makes a physical advance on Odintsova. On the previous day she had provoked a confession of love from Bazarov by responding to his announcement that he was going to leave with the admission that she would be bored in his absence. The physical attraction between them is palpable: Anna's face is pale, Bazarov's hands shake, and Anna seems to drink in Bazarov's reference to her beauty: "A secret agitation was overcoming her little by little. It was communicated to Bazarov" (133). The scene ends inconclusively with talk about love and yielding oneself. The next day, on the morning of his departure, Anna asks Bazarov to come to her room and renews the conversation of the previous evening. She seems to provoke a declaration of love by asking him about his reserve in expressing his feelings. He declares finally, "Know, then, that I love you—foolishly, madly" (141). She stretches out her hands, and Bazarov draws her forcefully into his arms. She does not free herself from his embrace immediately but then does with the words, "You have misunderstood me" (142).

This scene more than any other has contributed to the widespread notion that Anna is a flirt, selfishly and cynically prodding Bazarov toward a declaration of love for her own egotistic ends. The view would seem to have considerable merit, since Anna provokes him by words and gesture to make this declaration. A kinder and more sympathetic interpretation is possible, however. Anna is sincerely attracted to Bazarov; she is no idle flirt and wastes no time or extracts no specious and cheap profit from her relationship with the willing Arkady. Her interest in Bazarov is genuine, and his originality, intelligence, and differentness tempt her. She leads a narrow, sheltered, disciplined life, unfree in action but free in fantasy, and Bazarov is her fantasy—that it might be possible to love and be loved by a man of intelligence and talent. The two scenes in which she provokes his declaration of love and physical advances are a kind of tentative playing out of a fantasy of love for Bazarov.

Flirtation is too trivial a word for what Odintsova does. She goes as far as her nature permits her; she goes to the brink of her fantasy, but no further. Later she admits her fault with a candor we cannot attribute to Bazarov: "I too transgressed on that occasion, if not through coquetry then through something else" (238). That something else must be the momentary fantasy of living with feelings that went beyond the strict controls that she had set up for herself and that had been forced on her. In the end, she is more realistic and mature than Bazarov. First, she understands herself in a way that Bazarov never understands himself. She is not prepared to risk what her whole life had warned her against—love for and marriage to a penniless country doctor, whatever his prospects, with an impulsive and volatile nature. She had given her passion to one man, her father, and that passion had betrayed her—a misplacement of trust she had paid for with the unlove of another man. She might be tempted in fantasy to repeat the gamble, but she is too bright, sensitive, and mature to do so. She knows the difference between fantasy and reality, passion and love.

14

The Change in Bazarov

Odintsova's rejection of Bazarov has provoked an extreme change in him. Before the rejection Bazarov is strong, courageous, and sure of his beliefs; after it he becomes cynical, indifferent, listless, aimless, and despairing, and finally he seems to commit a passive suicide. The change is so great as to throw into question everything Bazarov stands for. The change is visible immediately after the scene of failed passion: he cannot sleep, eat, or smoke, and he is morose. His first reaction is to downgrade and castigate relations with women: working on a chain gang smashing stones is preferable to being in the clutches of a woman. He turns to the peasant driving the cart and asks him if his wife beats him, and when the peasant answers indignantly that this does not happen, Bazarov admits that this is what education brings one to—to be slapped down by a woman. He refers sarcastically to the peasant driver as a "sage" and generalizes about human life: "Every mortal is dangling on a thread, a bottomless gulf may spread out under him any minute but, besides that, he thinks up all sorts of unpleasant things for himself, he messes up his own life" (151).

During the visit to his parents Bazarov continues to reflect on the uselessness of life. The day after their arrival at his parents' home, Bazarov says to Arkady as the two lie in a hayrick,

The tiny narrow spot I'm taking up is so infinitesimally small by comparison with the rest of space, where I am not and which has nothing to do with me, and the portion of time which I may succeed in living through is so insignificant when confronted with eternity, wherein I was not and shall not be. Yet within this atom, this mathematical point, the blood is circulating, the brain is working, something or other yearns also to. . . . What hideous incongruity! What trifles! (173)

In the same scene Bazarov cheers on an ant dragging a dead fly. He tells Arkady that he hates many people, calling his friend wishy-washy. Arkady had also mentioned that Russia would attain perfection when the last peasant had as good a place to live in as did the overseer Philip. To this Bazarov says, "But me, I've grown to hate this ultimate *mouzhik*, this Philip or Sidor, for whom I am in duty bound to strain every nerve and sinew, and who won't give me as much as a thank-you; and besides, what would I do with his thank-you? Well, so he'll be living in that white hut, but I'll be pushing up the daisies" (176). He calls Pavel an idiot to Arkady. The scene ends with Bazarov, in a mock but half-serious attempt at murder, grabbing Arkady by the throat.

In this scene Bazarov is callous, contemptuous of man, concerned with the uselessness and triviality of life, and aggressive to his friend. He is far from the Bazarov of the first half of the novel. To be sure, he was then too aggressive, rude, and bad-mannered, but he was also filled with purpose and engrossed in work; he spoke to the peasant children with seriousness and concern. His mood and masochistic remarks can in part be explained by a bruised ego. When he is saying good-bye to Odintsova the last time he sees her at her estate, he says to Arkady, "An empty space turned up in the suitcase, and so I'm filling it with hay. That's just how it is with the suitcase of life: it doesn't matter what you stuff it with, as long as there is no emptiness" (250).

A kind of self-flagellation goes on, disguised, though not very deeply, by irony and aggression against others. Bazarov is merciless toward others and toward himself. Working for the welfare of others and especially for the peasants is a ridiculous idea; people resemble ants, the universe is something of a joke, and it is designed to humble brave and intelligent spirits like himself. To demean Odintsova is to mute the spiritual wreckage of Bazarov. But to read her more sympathetically, as I am convinced she must be, is to throw into even sharper relief how frail is the foundation on which rests the image of Bazarov as a self-possessed and intrepid defender of what is best for his fellow man. There seems to be no way we can escape the conclusion that Odintsova is stronger than he, that an essential insecurity, both of class and of psychology, is revealed in her presence. She demonstrates how quickly he cracks under a disappointment in himself and how quickly he is drained of purpose.

Clearly Odintsova had broken something in Bazarov, and that something goes to the very depths of his being. What is insistent in his actions and thoughts after the failure in love is self-aggression and images of desolation and death. The aggression he had turned against Pavel and others in the first part of the novel is now turned against himself. What he had externalized is now internalized. The social negation he had advanced in the first part becomes in the second part a personal negation. In the first part Bazarov had shown how purposeless and stupid were the lives of the gentry, particularly that of Pavel; in the second part he comes to believe that his own life is stupid and purposeless. He had believed that he and enlightened humanity could control the destinies of men. The love affair with Odintsova had compelled Bazarov to acknowledge forces within himself that override his will and his judgment. Bazarov had wanted to wipe the slate clean of authorities, but for Turgenev the slate is never clean. There are always natural authorities: love, death, birth, and the condition of man as something of an accident in an indifferent cosmos.

The change is so great that it is dismaying to find some critics who maintain that no change has taken place. A. V. Knowles is among these critics:

> After his experience with Odintsova, Bazarov might appear to be a different man from the one Turgenev depicted before their fateful meeting. But he is not. Rather, he has found some of his convictions wanting, and for the first time in his life is at a loss. But his reaction is in no sense out of character. Nor is his retreat afterward to his parental home in any way surprising. Odintsova has revealed to him an aspect of his personality of which he had

previously been unaware. He had denied the power of love (or even its existence) before he had encountered it, just as he had denied everything else. He then accepts his discovery, however unfortunate for him it may be. His empiricism lasts to the very end. (Knowles, 176)

Such a defense seems to come from the readiness of many critics to brook no serious criticism of Bazarov. It overlooks the very profound change in his purpose in life and respect for others.

P. G. Pustovojt has had the honesty and courage to confront fully Odintsova's devasting effect on Bazarov. He sees the change and states it starkly: "Up to chapter 14, in which Bazarov makes the acquaintance of Odintsova, that is, where Bazarov's basic plot is formed, Bazarov is a sober and intelligent person, who believes in himself and what he is doing and who is free of skepticism, pessimism: he is proud, sure of his goals and capable not only of influencing others, but of overpowering them with his knowledge, logic and will" (Pustovojt, 176). But there is a decisive change, and Bazarov becomes the opposite: "The hero does not succeed in remaining what he was before he met Odintsova. The wound is deep and he remains in despair to the end of the novel" (176). Bazarov cannot overcome in himself "the feelings of spite, spiritual bankruptcy, irritation and despair." Pustovojt is at loss to explain the cause of such despair and believes it is inconceivable that it could come from love alone. In some deep and basic sense he is right: the rejection by Odintsova triggered feelings of self-contempt and loss of purpose that must have been there from the very beginning. This is not to say that "love" is not a substantial cause in itself. It is, after all, an emotion that is intimately tied in our minds to self-worth, and nowhere more so than in Turgenev's view of life. But if so, then there must have been a predisposition in Bazarov to feel unloved.

In any event Bazarov's whole intellectual scaffolding is insufficient to protect him from the loss of self-worth that he feels as a consequence of the Odintsova affair. All his contempt for emotions and his reduction of men's feelings to physiological impulses are called into question by his own failure to live by them. The impulse of many to protect Bazarov against the failure in love by denigrating Odintsova, or denying that any substantial change has taken place, may be a defense of something more important to them: the structure of ideas and positions that Bazarov embodies in the first half of the novel. The positive, strong Bazarov, who is the enemy of social lethargy and obscurantism and the champion of a bold new vision of life, is a Bazarov too attractive for most critics to abandon to the truth of his nature. One could, of course, salvage Bazarov's position by separating it from the man: the vision is beautiful, but the man is inadequate. But few have tried to follow this dubious logic. It is even possible that Turgenev himself could not come to the unsettling conclusion about Bazarov. The truth of his artistic logic may have led him to truths that, as a man, he had difficulty accepting.

In this changed mood of contempt for his fellow man and despair about the purpose of life Bazarov lends himself to the duel with Pavel over Fenechka. A duel is a ritual associated with the aristocratic life of Pavel and something that Bazarov looks on with derision. On his return to Maryino, Arkady's father's estate, Bazarov returns to his work with seriousness. He gives up his arguments with Pavel, and a kind of uneasy truce is established between them. Bazarov attempts to take up the activity that sustained him before his meeting with Odintsova. His irony does not leave him, and he is afflicted with a certain restlessness.

It is in this mood that Bazarov's attention turns increasingly to Fenechka. She feels at ease with him and consults him frequently about her baby. He meets her one morning in a lilac arbor as she sits on a bench arranging white and red roses she had just plucked. Bazarov turns the conversation repeatedly to comments on her beauty: "The tip of your little nose moves ever so charmingly when you read" (202); "I love it when you talk. It's just like a rill pourling" (202); "All the clever ladies in the world aren't worth the dimple on your little elbow" (203). The conversation then turns playfully to payment for Bazarov's ministrations to the little baby. Bazarov first asks for payment by a rose and then manipulates Fenechka into a position in which he kisses her. It is difficult to read this scene without discomfort; it is so trite and commonplace and so out of keeping with the brave and resolute Bazarov of the first part of the novel. Even more, it is morally irresponsible of him to take advantage of his position as a guest, doctor, and friend by making a physical advance to her. Indeed, he acts in the same way he had earlier condemned the aristocrats as acting—by exercising a kind of *droit du seigneur* toward someone from the peasant class.

Why does he act in such a reprehensible manner? Probably in part from the mood of cynicism that has settled on him since his rejection by Odintsova, and in some sense from an attempt to rehabilitate himself vis-à-vis women. This is suggested in the following: "Bazarov recalled another recent scene and he became both ashamed and contemptuously vexed" (205). It is even possible that in some obscure way he wishes to avenge himself against women and chooses the hapless and innocent Fenechka for this purpose. Whatever the cause, there would seem no justification of his action. In view of the stupid and foolish way that Bazarov acts in the flirtation and duel, it is difficult to understand Richard Freeborn's defense of Bazarov in this embarrassing scene: "Yet the fact that they fight the duel ostensibly over Fenechka, the peasant girl, shows the way in which the ideological issues are welded into the structure of the novel. For Bazarov's readiness to fight the duel must be understood in the light of the fact that he is prepared not only to reject the dvoryanstvo [gentry], but also to devote his life to working for the peasants" (Freeborn, 72).

There is nothing in this embarrassing scene, in which Bazarov takes advantage of young peasant girl's trust in him as a doctor to kiss her and to trifle with her affections in the most banal way, that would suggest that it can be read to his credit as in some way working for the peasants. Turgenev seems to suggest that Bazarov must accept the duel, because otherwise Pavel would have resorted to beating him with a stick. If this were true, however, how do we account for his self-mocking and cynical exaggeration of the romantic situation he has thrust himself into? The first Bazarov would have brushed off Pavel's challenge with some scornful remark. Bazarov's flirtation with and stealing of a kiss from Fenechka and his acceptance of the duel all seem a voluntary immersion of himself in what he had held in the highest scorn, and it is in keeping with his self-flagellation after the Odintsova episode.

The Change in Bazarov

Bazarov has lost faith in himself, or he has discovered a weakness and deals with it by exaggerating that weakness. If he is not what he thought he was, he will be worse than he is. On the morning of the duel Bazarov constantly repeats to himself "how foolish." During the preparations for the duel and during the duel itself, he maintains a mocking tone, indicating his distance from the matter as serious even while he indulges in it. He says to Pavel, "Why not laugh and blend *utile dulci*—the useful with the agreeable? That's it, then: you let me have bite in French, and I'll let you have it in Latin" (214). Pavel perceives the mockery but lets it go. Bazarov tells Pavel that Peter can act as a second and Bazarov will coach him in the proper mannerism of a second, especially since he stands on the peak of contemporary culture. Peter is a house serf who, having absorbed some of the superficial mannerisms of gentility, is a parody of serious culture.

This is another item in the long feud between him and Pavel, but whereas Bazarov had easily bested Pavel on the ideological front, we are tempted to see Pavel as coming out better in this scene. To be sure, he acts in accordance with his inflexible principles and, in our view, overreacts to a trivial scene. He is apparently protecting his brother's honor. Bazarov, on the other hand, acts irresponsibly, especially as a guest at the estate. The best defense of Bazarov would seem to be that he indulges in the flirtation, the kiss, and the duel as a kind of ironic and contemptuous imitation of the way the masters behave. He seems to be aware that he is acting stupidly, and in that sense he rises a bit over the action.

His suggestion, too, that they speak in Latin at the duel is another item of self-conscious ironic contempt for the traditional rituals of the gentry. Still, the idea that he indulges in this charade as a way of laughing, in imitation, at the masters does not seem to wash. He knows there to be no audience when he indulges in the flirtation and kiss—at least he is not aware that Pavel is watching. Pavel, on the other hand, seems somewhat justified in "punishing" a guest who has overstepped the proprieties of the house. There is one other consideration in understanding this curious finale to Pavel and Bazarov's relations, and that is the possibility that both men are physically attracted to Fenechka. There was earlier the enigmatic scene in which Pavel enters the room of Fenechka to ask her to order tea and her discomfort before his questions. After the duel and while he is in bed, Pavel draws Nikolay's attention to the fact that Fenechka looks like Nellie, his Princess R. And in his delirium he says, "Ah, how I love this insignificant being" (220), apparently referring to Fenechka. Bazarov concludes that Pavel is in love with Fenechka, but he does not seem aware that the same may be true of him. Bazarov had been rebuffed by Odintsova in his sexual advance, and his bruised ego may be solacing itself by the flirtation with Fenechka. If that is so, then it speaks badly of his character.

As Bazarov bandages Pavel's leg and Peter has been sent off to get water, the two men fall into an uncomfortable intimacy, suggesting that they have something in common. Given the vitriolic exchanges and profound differences between them on almost every ideological issue, such a similarity would seem surprising, to say the least. Pisarev has said that the two men were similar in the cast of their mind, meaning that both were proud, stubborn, and determined to make their views prevail. David Lowe has added to this the fact that they both undergo personality changes because of a woman—namely, Princess R. and Odintsova. Both men are attracted to Fenechka, and Fenechka reminds Pavel of Princess R. and Bazarov of Odintsova. In a dream Bazarov has the night before the duel, Fenechka in the form of a cat trails after Odintsova, making the connection explicit between the events that lead him to indulge in the duel and his love for Odintsova. Princess R. had broken something in Pavel, so that his life was drained of purpose and meaning, and Odintsova had done the same to Bazarov.

Lowe raises another important issue when he says that "the conflicts in the novel are the results of difference or similarities in temperament, with political ideology relegated to an inferior role" (Lowe, 38). It is astonishing to say that political ideology has an inferior role for these two, given that a good part of the novel is an ideological collision between the two. It is also astonishing to say that personality has the dominant role. One need not choose, because personality and ideology are not separate but deeply intertwined. Would this imply, then, that Pavel and Bazarov, since they share similar personality traits, are not wholly at different ideological poles? Not in content, certainly, for their worldviews are starkly different: one is oriented toward the past, the other toward the future; one favors the aristocracy, the other democracy. But Pavel's traditional ideology and Bazarov's radical "future" ideology are, like these men's personalities, alike in an important way: both are closed ideologies in that they are finished in conception and impervious to change; both are "willed" ideologies, no matter what the difference in content, in that they assume that the world must answer to their conceptions of it.

Love as a mysterious passion, passing beyond the control and reason of the participants, is considered by Bazarov to be a self-inflicted and stupid mysticism. Love as a mysterious passion passing beyond the control of reason is something that Pavel accepts and lives by. Despite the difference in beliefs, both men have suffered a similar fate. The Odintsova affair has shown Bazarov that he is not exempt from passions he had considered foolish and useless, and his defense against them is to exaggerate them. Bazarov seems to be saying, "I'm no better than Pavel, so I might as well act as he does."

It is no accident that while the nonsense of the duel is going on, the real life of love, marriage, work, and child-bearing goes on without Pavel and Bazarov: during the same period Arkady and Katya are falling in love, and Nikolay is working. When the novel ends Bazarov has departed in death and Pavel in absence, but Nikolay and Arkady have been reunited in a double wedding. In Turgenev's conservatism, he gives life and continuity to those who acknowledge the traditional values of marriage, child-bearing, and work. Turgenev understood that the fulcrum of the radicals' platform lay precisely in their claim that man could take command of life—his own and others'—by way of will and reason, and it is precisely this fulcrum that Turgenev is at pains to topple.

15

Bazarov's Death

Bazarov's death is senseless. He dies from an accidental cut and from the slovenly methods and instruments of a provincial doctor. After he leaves Odintsova and is in the grip of pessimism and cynicism he retires to his father's small estate. He intends to work, but in a short time he finds himself unable to. He is restless and bored and apparently still morose. He has lost his direction and sense of purpose, and what characterizes his presence at his parents' home is an aimless wandering. He follows his father in his rounds and seems to need company. Responding to his father's suggestion that with the imminent serf emancipation Russia is progressing, Bazarov voices cynicism about progress. And he seeks out peasants to prove to himself how ignorant and undeserving they are to be the symbols of Russia's progress. Bazarov cuts himself accidentally while assisting at an autopsy on a peasant who had died of typhus. The attending doctor did not have anything to cauterize the wound, and by the time Bazarov is able to cauterize the wound it is too late. As a consequence this talented, intelligent, progressive youth, who easily towers above all the other characters in the novel in intelligence and abilities, is cut down senselessly.

Bazarov's Death

We must ask why it is that Turgenev reserved such a fate for Bazarov and what the meaning of this fate has for the novel. This question cannot be answered without relating it to the other important question: Why does Turgenev take his hero from the confident, brusque, buoyant representative of the best of Russia and have him develop—apparently by way of his failed love with Odintsova—into a pessimistic, despairing, purposeless, and ultimately self-destructive person? Bazarov's drastic change in mood and purpose culminates in his death; he commits a passive suicide that is prepared for by his loss of faith in himself. Even before he returns to his parents his language is filled with images of death and destruction. Would someone as intelligent and self-possessed as Bazarov permit himself to be so careless as to cut himself at an autopsy? Indeed, why does he participate in the autopsy of an infected patient without taking the proper precautions? And why does he wait four hours to cauterize his wound? Turgenev seems to be saying that Bazarov's death is the culmination of his loss of faith in himself.

Bazarov's death has been received by critics as a coronation of his stature and humanity. They see Bazarov as a fearless and broadly talented young man struck down before his promise can be realized. Many refer to his "tragic death," having in mind the contrast between the immense promise of a young man and the indifferent and casual way in which he is cut down. In addition, Bazarov's conduct during his last days in the face of inevitable death is seen by most as consonant with his strong character. It is true that Bazarov never tries to hide from the facts; he does not whine, rail against the injustice of the universe, or indulge in illusions about cures. His attitude toward death may be fruitfully contrasted with the attitude of Ivan Ilyich in Tolstoy's famous novel *The Death of Ivan Ilyich* (1887). Ivan Ilyich tries to deny the inevitability of death, blames others, rails against God and the universe, indulges in all kinds of illusory cures, and is generally unpleasant to his friends and his family. Bazarov, on the other hand, softens in his emotions toward his parents and Odintsova. He stares at the abyss without flinching. His only appeal to emotion is to ask his father to send for Odintsova.

Odintsova comes and brings a doctor with her. It is perhaps in keeping with her rational and practical nature that she would come at the bequest of a beloved friend and yet not lose sight of the practical side of her errand. Her rapid response to his appeal is undoubtedly some gesture to the emotion, if not the love, she had felt for Bazarov, as well as evidence of her humane nature. The doctor cannot do anything, but Odintsova can bring some solace to the last moments of someone she had admired. Bazarov tells her that he loves her. Odintsova shudders at these words—ambiguously perhaps because they touch something in her, or perhaps because she is chilled and frightened by the sight of the dying man. It has been pointed out by critics not well-disposed toward Odintsova that she gives Bazarov a glass of water without taking off her glove, as if she were afraid of contracting the disease. This may be so, because she is a deliberate and circumspect individual. On the other hand, she kisses his forehead.

What is Turgenev saying in having his hero die in such a senseless way? In the first part of the novel he gives Bazarov respect, purpose, and intelligence and makes him the representative of the best of Russia's future. In the second half of the novel he humbles him, robs him of a sense of purpose, and turns him to death. In a 26 April 1862 letter to K. K. Sluchevsky, Turgenev wrote, "I wanted to make him a tragic figure—tenderness was not the point. He is honest, true, and a democrat to the end of his fingertips" (185). In the same letter he also wrote, "If the reader does not come to like Bazarov with all his coarseness, callousness, pitiless dryness, and harshness—if you do not come to love him, I repeat—then I am at fault and did not reach my goal" (186). Also, "I dreamed of a gloomy, wild, huge figure, half-sprung from the earth, strong, sardonic, honest—and yet fated for destruction because he stands at the threshold of the future" (186). Turgenev seems to be saying in the last quotation that Bazarov dies because he represents something that cannot exist in the present "because he stands at the threshold of the future." This is an enigmatic explanation of his death and not entirely clear, and it is indeed out of keeping with the aimlessness and despair of Bazarov's last days.

Turgenev's comments on Bazarov are not all of one piece. For the most part, he tended to identify with Bazarov, and in one letter said that he identified with all of Bazarov's views except those on art. But on occasion Turgenev confessed to not knowing whether he admired Bazarov, as he did in an 18 April 1862 letter to Fet: "Did I want to abuse Bazarov or praise him? *I myself don't know* because I don't know whether or not I like him or hate him!" (184). The novel does not, however, support admiration. Bazarov is not someone who "stands at the threshold of the future," who is somehow punished for his advanced views. It is true, at least from the retrospective position of the late twentieth century, that Bazarov's unsentimental view of the gentry and class privilege, his pragmatic nature, his worship of science, his criticism of tradition and mysticism, and his championing of reason and work will continue to strike many as advanced views at the "threshold of the future."

The novel seems to complicate these statements, because it expresses Turgenev's profound ambiguity toward Bazarov. Turgenev destroys the symbol of the future and celebrates the continuity of conservative forces. Between Bazarov and Pavel, Turgenev seems to choose the middle way. Both Pavel and Bazarov leave Russia, one by death and the other by emigrating and leading a life useless and irrelevant to Russia's future. The Kirsanovs, however, seem to represent for Turgenev what he seems to say Russia needs: continuity, work, family, and the middle way. Pavel, Odintsova, and Bazarov leave nothing for Russia. None has children, whereas Nikolay bridges the gap between peasant and gentry not by words or theories but by marriage and children. And Arkady, once he has sloughed off the student carapace of radical thought weakly assimilated, returns to the world of his father. He marries Katya, tills the soil, and remains attached to his ancestral roots.

Bazarov, Turgenev seems to say, had rejected all authorities and believed that man, by his self-motivated reason and will, could create a new society. But Turgenev also seems to be saying that there are authorities that everyone must accept: death, love, and the mysterious processes of nature. Bazarov and his radical real-life prototypes believed in a world to be created by reason and will, and Turgenev says that there are forces greater and more powerful than reason and will. Indeed, he seems to say that reason and will, abstracted from the concrete process of life, are destructive.

Notes

1. Vissarion G. Belinsky (1811–48), the father of Russian criticism, discovered and championed such writers as Dostoyevski, Turgenev, Gogol, and Lermontov. Alexander Herzen (1812–70) was the most important Russian social thinker of the nineteenth century, living most of his life outside Russia. He edited the important émigré newspaper *The Bell* from 1857 to 1861. T. N. Granovsky (1813–55) was a liberal historian satirized by Dostoyevski in *The Possessed*.

2. N. K. Chernyshevsky (1828–89), the most important of the radical critics, was a philosopher, literary critic, and political activist. Nikolay A. Drobolyubov (1836–61), an intellectual literary critic during the 1850s, was a disciple of Chernyshevsky's and in the eyes of many the prototype of Bazarov. The critic, intellectual, and activist Dmitri I. Pisarev (1840–68) was in some respects the most radical of the group around Chernyshevsky.

3. An English translation of this 1867 essay can be found in the Norton Critical Edition of *Fathers and Sons*, ed. Ralph Matlaw (New York: Norton, 1966). This essay and other critical pieces from the Norton edition of the novel are hereafter cited in text.

4. An English translation of this piece can be found in *Belinsky, Chernyshevsky, and Dobrolyubov*, ed. Ralph Matlaw (New York: Dutton, 1962); hereafter cited in text.

5. Alexander Herzen, "Bazarov Once Again." A translation of this essay can be found in the Norton edition of *Fathers and Sons*.

6. See N. N. Strakhov, *Kriticheskije stat'i: Otssy i deti* (Kiev, 1908). First published in *Time* in April 1862. See the partial translation in the Norton edition of *Fathers and Sons*, 218–19.

7. Dmitri Pisarev's article "Bazarov" was published in 1862. Translated by Lydia Hooke in the Norton edition of *Fathers and Sons* (the translation is not complete but not indicated as such); hereafter cited in text.

Notes

8. David Lowe, *Turgenev's "Fathers and Sons"* (Ann Arbor, Mich.: Ardis, 1983); hereafter cited in text.

9. Victor Ripp, *Turgenev's Russia* (Ithaca, N.Y.: Cornell University Press, 1980); hereafter cited in text.

10. Letter of 9 October from P. V. Annenkov to Turgenev. A translation of this letter can be found in the Norton edition of *Fathers and Sons*. All Turgenev's letters in this edition are hereafter cited in text.

11. Isaiah Berlin, *Fathers and Children* (Oxford: Clarendon Press, 1972), 29; hereafter cited in text.

12. René Wellek, "Fathers and Sons," in the Norton edition of *Fathers and Sons*, 260; hereafter cited in text.

13. P. G. Pustovojt, *Ottsy i deti i ideinaia bor'ba 60-x godov XIX* (Moscow: Proveshchenie, 1964), 177. This important work has not been translated but is discussed at some length in Edward Wasiolek, "Bazarov and Odintsova," *Canadian-American Slavic Studies* 17, no. 1 (Spring 1983); hereafter cited in text.

14. Joel Blair, "The Architecture of Turgenev's *Fathers and Sons*," *Modern Fiction Studies* 19, no. 4 (Winter 1973–74): 559; hereafter cited in text.

15. Eva Kagan-Kans, *Hamlet and Don Quixote: Turgenev's Ambivalent Vision* (The Hague: Mouton, 1975); hereafter cited in text.

16. In the 1983 article "Bazarov and Odintsova."

17. Edward Garnett, *Turgenev* (London: Collins Press, 1917), 179; hereafter cited in text.

18. Richard Freeborn, *Turgenev, the Novelist's Novelist* (London: Oxford University Press, 1960), 74; hereafter cited in text.

19. A. V. Knowles, *Ivan Turgenev* (Boston: Twayne Publishers, 1988), 80; hereafter cited in text.

20. Ralph Matlaw, "Turgenev's Novels and *Fathers and Sons*," in the Norton edition of the novel, 278.

21. Gary Jahn, "Character and Theme in *Fathers and Sons*," *College Literature* 4, no. 1 (Winter 1977): 86; hereafter cited in text.

22. For references to James's laudatory opinion of Turgenev, see his introductory essay on Turgenev in *Memoirs of a Sportsman*, trans. I. Hapgood, in *The Novels and Stories of Ivan Turgenieff*, vol. 1 (New York: Scribners, 1903). See also Henry James, "Turgenev and Tolstoy," in *The Art of the Novel*, ed. Leon Edel (New York: Vintage, 1956). Also Dale E. Peterson, *Clement Vision* (Port Washington, N.Y.: Kennikat Press, 1975).

23. John A. T. Lloyd, *Ivan Turgenev* (1942; Port Washington, N.Y.: Kennikat Press, 1972).

24. See *Hamlet and Don Quixote*, trans. Robert Nichols (Norwood, Pa.: Norwood Editions, 1974), 12, and Kagan-Kans, *Hamlet and Don Quixote*.

Notes

25. From chapter 33 of Turgenev's *On the Eve*.

26. D. S. Mirsky, *A History of Russian Literature* (London: George Routledge & Sons, 1927).

27. Dmitri Pisarev, *The Destruction of Aesthetics* (1865; Moscow: GosIz KhLit, 1965). This important work is not available in English, but discussion of it can be found in Wasiolek, "Bazarov and Odintsova." For a selection of Pisarev's essays in English (excluding "Bazarov" and "The Destruction of Aesthetics") see *Selected Philosophical, Social, and Political Essays*, ed. Ralph Matlaw (New York: Dutton, 1962).

Selected Bibliography

Primary Works

The Works of I. Turgenieff. Translated by Isabel Hapgood. 12 vols. Boston and New York: Jefferson, 1903.

The Novels and Stories of Ivan Turgenieff. Translated by I. Hapgood. 15 vols. New York: Scribners, 1903. Introductory essay by Henry James in the first volume.

Fathers and Sons. Translated by Bernard Guilbert Guerney. New York: The Modern Library, 1961.

Fathers and Sons. Edited by Ralph Matlaw; translated by Constance Garnett with substantial changes by the editor. New York: Norton, 1966. A fine companion edition to Guerney's translation. It does not read as well as Guerney's, but much of the appendix material (particularly the primary sources) is a good auxiliary to the novel.

Secondary Works

Books

Berlin, Isaiah. *Fathers and Children.* Oxford: Clarendon, 1972. Short (62-page) volume concerned primarily with the novel's ideological background and reception.

Fitzlyon, April. *The Price of Genius: The Life of Pauline Viardot.* London: Calder, 1964. Well-done biography of Turgenev's mistress and an overview of her career in the context of the times.

Freeborn, Richard. *Turgenev, the Novelist's Novelist*. Oxford: Oxford University Press, 1960. An overview of Turgenev's work, paying special attention to Turgenev's four great novels under such rubrics as "Structure," "Ideas and Ideals," "Hero and Heroine," and "Achievement."

Garnett, Edward. *Turgenev: A Study*. Foreword by Joseph Conrad. London: Collins, 1917. Conrad's Foreword is interesting. Good source for an early English view of Turgenev. Ecstatic view of Bazarov.

Gettman, R. A. *Turgenev in England and America*. Urbana: University of Illinois Press, 1941.

Kagan-Kans, Eva. *Hamlet and Don Quixote: Turgenev's Ambivalent Vision*. The Hague: Mouton, 1975.

Lloyd, John A. T. *Ivan Turgenev*. 1942. Port Washington, N.Y., and London: Kennikat, 1972. Pleasantly written with incidental biography and commentary on the major novels.

Lowe, David. *Turgenev's "Fathers and Sons."* Ann Arbor: Ardis, 1983. A balanced treatment of the novel; sees *Fathers and Sons* as a "comedy" according to Northrop Frye's definition.

Magarshack, David. *Turgenev: A Life*. London: Faber, 1954. Biography with some historical background chapters on such intellectual figures as Bakunin, Stankevich, Belinsky, and Herzen. Minimal commentary on the novels. *Father and Sons* is dealt with by way of critical reaction to it.

Matlaw, Ralph, ed. *Belinsky, Chernyshevsky, and Dobrolyubov: Selective Criticism*. New York: Dutton, 1962. A good English-language source of articles by these important radicals.

Moser, Charles. *Ivan Turgenev*. New York: Columbia University Press, 1972.

Paperno, Irina. *Chernyshevsky and the Age of Realism*. Stanford, Calif.: Stanford University Press, 1988. Chernyshevsky was an important influence on Turgenev, especially on his *Fathers and Sons*, and this is a good study of the man and his work.

Peterson, Dale E. *The Clement Vision: Poetic Realism in Turgenev and James*. Port Washington, N.Y.: Kennikat, 1975. Thorough treatment of this important relationship.

Pritchett, V. S. *The Gentle Barbarian*. New York: Vintage, 1977. Well-written biography with considerable insight into the works. Very readable.

Ripp, Victor. *Turgenev's Russia from "Notes of a Hunter" to "Fathers and Sons."* Ithaca, N.Y.: Cornell University Press, 1980. Study of Turgenev's four major novels in the context of the social situation of the time. Ripp is particularly concerned with the rift between official values and the values of the educated elite.

Schapiro, Leonard. *Turgenev: His Life and Times*. New York: Random House, 1978. A biography with a chapter on the radicals' reaction to the novel.

Selected Bibliography

Troyat, Henri. *Turgenev*, translated by Nancy Amphoux. New York: Dutton, 1985. Pleasant reading, but written as "imaginative" biography in which matters are re-created on a slight factual basis. Pritchett's biography is more reliable.

Waddington, Patrick. *Turgenev and England*. New York: New York University Press, 1981.

Zhitova, V. *The Turgenev Family*, translated by A. S. Mills. London: Harvell Press, 1948. Eye-witness account of the Turgenev family from a ward of Turgenev's mother.

Articles and Parts of Books

Blair, Joel. "The Architecture of Turgenev's *Fathers and Sons*." *Modern Fiction Studies* 19, no. 4 (Winter 1973–74): 555–63. A satisfactory but conventional view.

Fischler, Alexlander. "The Garden Motif and the Structure of Turgenev's *Fathers and Sons*." *Novel* 9 (1976): 245–55.

Howe, Irving. "Turgenev: The Politics of Hesitation." In *Politics and the Novel*, 114–38. London: Stevens, 1961. Excellent piece.

Jahn, Gary R. "Character and Theme in *Fathers and Sons*." *College Literature* 4, no. 1 (1977): 80–91. A substantially different view of the relations between Bazarov and Odintsova from what is presented in this volume.

Lowe, David A. "Comedy and Tragedy in *Fathers and Sons*: A Structural Analysis." *Canadian-American Slavic Studies* 43, no. 3 (1979): 283–94.

Reeve, F. D. "Fathers and Children." In *The Russian Novel*, 119–58. New York: McGraw-Hill, 1978. An imaginative and novel interpretation.

Wasiolek, Edward. "Bazarov and Odintsova." *Canadian-American Slavic Studies* 17, no. 1 (Spring 1983): 39–48.

Index

Index

"Hamlet and Don Quixote," 28, 29–32
Hegel, Friedrich, 3, 33, 83, 84
Hemingway, Ernest, 52, 53, 54
Herzen, Alexander, 4, 11, 12, 13

Jahn, Gary, 19
James, Henry, 20, 52, 54

Kagan-Kans, Eva, 15
Katkov, Mikhail, 5, 11
Knowles, A. V., 17, 18, 19, 103, 104

Liszt, Franz, 93
Lloyd, A. T., 20
Lowe, David, 14, 108

Macaulay, Thomas, 87
Matlaw, Ralph, 18
Michelet, Jules, 87
Mirsky, D. S., 57
Musset, Alfred de, 93

A Nest of Gentlefolk, 47, 56, 93
Nicholas I, 3
Notes of a Hunter, 21, 22

On the Eve, 32, 48, 56, 93

Peter the Great, 5
Pisarev, Dmitri, 5, 13, 18, 23, 61, 75, 78, 79, 108
Proudhon, Pierre-Joseph, 87
Pushkin, Alexander, 79; *Gypsies*, 72
Pustovojt, P. G., 15, 16, 91, 104

Raphael, 72
raznochinsty, 4, 61
Ripp, Victor, 15, 18, 19, 20
Rudin, 47, 48, 50, 55, 56, 93

Sand, George, 93
Schiller, Friedrich, 68
Slavophiles, 67
Sluchevsky, K. K., 12, 112
Strakhov, N. N., 5, 12, 13, 17, 18

Tolstoy, Leo, 5, 8, 12; *The Death of Ivan Ilyich*, 111; *War and Peace*, 6, 8; *What Is Art*, 35, 79
Twain, Mark, *Huckleberry Finn*, 7

utopian socialism, 41

Wellek, René, 15, 17, 18
Westerners, 67

The Author

Edward Wasiolek is Distinguished Service Professor of English, Slavic, and Comparative Literature at the University of Chicago. He holds a Ph.D. from Harvard University and has been a visiting professor at the University of Indiana, Northwestern University, the University of Illinois, Carleton College, and Harvard University. He is the author of critical works on Tolstoy and Dostoyevski and is the translator and editor of five volumes of Dostoyevski's notebooks. He has also published on such authors as Mark Twain, William Faulkner, Henry James, Joseph Conrad, and Jonathan Swift, as well as on various critical and theoretical subjects.